TALES OF A LAKELAND GYPSY

She

based on a series of stories told by
John Townsley,
a white faced Gypsy

Mill Field Publications

Tales of a Lakeland Gypsy

By the Same Author

A Lakes Christmas
Tales of a Lakeland Poacher
Tales of a Lakeland Valley - Buttermere
Tales of a Lakeland Valley - Borrowdale

Co author with Pat Evans
Tales of a Lakeland Valley - Loweswater

Copyright of text and photographs
Sheila Richardson 1996

ISBN 0 9526665 3 7

Published by
MILL FIELD PUBLICATIONS
8 Everest Mount, Workington, Cumbria
CA14 5 BY

CONTENTS

Tales of a Lakeland Gypsy

Acknowledgements

The author wishes to acknowledge the help and co - operation received from;

The Cumberland and Westmorland Antiquarian and Archeological Society for permission to quote from Oliver Wood's "West Cumbrian Coal".

Hopes Auction, Wigton.

Mr Robert Kelly, Malton, Yorkshire, for information on Gypsy funerals.

Mr W Rollinson, for permission to quote from his book, "Life and Tradition in the Lake District."

Mr Denis Wildridge, Workington for the use of photographs on pages 78, 91 & 97.

The West Cumberland Times and Star, Workington for permission to use the photograph on page 48.

The anonymous Travellers at Appleby Fair.

Mrs Kath Townsley, of Cockermouth.

Mr John Townsley, whose original manuscript has made this book possible

The information given to, and received by the author
has been done so in good faith.
No responsibility can be accepted by the author for any mis - understanding,
mis - representation, or mis - interpretation of any part of the text. Confirmation of
source material has been made wherever possible.

Introduction

John Townsley is a Cumbrian man who is proud of his Romany family heritage. He is descended from a long line of travellers who journeyed through Scotland and the north of England, dealing in horses, hawking goods, and turning their hands to anything that would make a penny.

John, his brother and six sisters, were the children of a marriage that joined together two of the great, long established Gypsy families in the country. His father was a Townsley, a family who originally came from Scotland, while his mother was a Cumbrian Lowther. Among his ancestors on the maternal side, John claims relationship many generations back, with a branch of the titled family that still hold that office in the county today.

John can be described as a "white faced Gypsy". This term distinguishes his pale complexion and sandy hair, from the swarthy faced, dark haired individuals that are the general conception of what a Gypsy should look like. Too many characterisations of this type-cast image of fiction writing have probably contributed to this idea, but truth, if not actually being stranger than fiction, is often more interesting.

John grew up in his west Cumbrian home to listen to tales about his Gypsy forebears from his parents and grandparents. *"There was nothing else to do on a winter's night, except gather round the fire and listen to the tales that the elders told us."*

While some of the facts about the adventures of his ancestors provided a cornerstone to record his family history, it is inevitable that with the passing of time, and numerous retellings by different relatives, the tales have passed from history into the realms of folk lore and legend. Young John Townsley listened, he learned and eventually followed their ways of dealing, and as a result, there were occasions when he sailed close to the legal wind.

He worked hard throughout his life, for even as a young lad of five, he was made to appreciate that work was the doctrine by which his family lived and survived. Even when he was drafted into the army for his six years of service during the second world war, *"I always did what the army wanted me to do, but I made sure that I worked for myself on the side."*

He grew up in an age when horses were essential to the business of every day life; from the delivery of such basic essentials as milk and coal, to the use of gigs and traps for personal transport. There was a wealth of knowledge about horses in the Family, of which John took advantage and as a result he became a good judge of horses and their potential value, and a skilful driver and handler.

With the decline of horse power after the second world war, he had to adapt his dealing skills to other sources. He eventually developed his own scrap business, virtually building it up from nothing. Earlier dealings in the traditional Gypsy way had made him alert enough to be aware of the possibilities of many dodges and fiddles that were to be tapped in industry and business, and he was eager to be among it. He

Tales of a Lakeland Gypsy

quickly became aware of how a few powerful and unscrupulous business people could virtually control a town, and in the course of this, buy their own legal protection.

John Townsley lived by his wits and earned a reputation for being a shrewd but fair dealer. He would always "pay the asking price", secure in the knowledge that he would eventually be able to make something out of it for himself. In this respect, he was something of a psychologist, for he was aware that people do not like to be proven ignorant, or wrong in their dealings. He went along with their suggestions and prices, even though he was aware at the time that they were undervaluing what they had to sell. He smiled at their satisfaction in the deals made to the reassuring rustle of bank notes.

John acknowledges that he has an ability to identify those people who are eager to "feather their own nests". When asked how he was able to recognise such people, he paused before replying; *"I suppose it's a sort of gift. I knew I could do business with them, and they knew they could do business with me. We just homed in on each other."*

During the course of his own business life, John Townsley made sufficient money to create a luxurious life-style for himself and his wife. He was able to "pay cash on the nail" for a fleet of Volvo trucks, and he rode around in the best of cars. He drove home from completing deals in many different parts of the country with up to £10,000 pounds in notes stuffed into his trousers. *"I was the first man in Cockermouth to own a new Jaguar"* he claimed proudly.

Since he gave up his scrap business, John and his wife Kath have taken the opportunity to travel the world. They have Romany friends and relatives in a number of different countries, and have visited many of them. *"When there is a big Romany wedding or funeral, there's no special invitations. Almost a thousand of the best known Romany families just converge."*

They have cruised on the QE 2 and rubbed shoulders with members of the old aristocracy and the nouveau riche. But John has never, ever forgotten his Romany background. *"Some Gypsies get above themselves. They make a lot of money and do well for themselves, then they don't want their friends to know what they've done to make their money, or who they were."*

. He now lives modestly with his wife Kath in a small, but comfortable flat. The Jaguars and Range Rovers have gone, for John is now content to get value for money by purchasing a second hand car from an auction. *"I was offered over the odds for my other car, a Ford, I couldn't turn the price down."*

Once a dealer, always a dealer, and while the trappings of an opulent life style may have been discarded as easily as an insect sheds its skin, the memories of his former life style remain. In the sitting room of his cosy home, John is surrounded by photographs of his wagons and horses, reminders of former successes in business and the show ring. Alongside are family mementoes of wealthy and important members of his family, about which he talks with pride.

John doesn't go out much now, he prefers to stay at home, recording his memories

Tales of a Lakeland Gypsy

in blue biro script over pages of many notebooks. He scribbles erratically, as the memories suddenly come to mind.

"I don't drink, and I don't smoke. Sitting in a pub listening to what fellas have been getting up to with other women is not for me. I like to have a crack about the old times, but nobody seems to want to listen."

John must have thought that I was a person to listen, for a telephone call informed me that he had something in which I could be interested. That something was a thick file of loose leaved pages, and an even thicker A4 sized notebook. The pages were covered with his sprawling block capital script. Contained within were the bare bones of fascinating stories of legendary travelling men, of wheeling and dealing, and hawking and horses. Sometimes the stories were left, half finished, to suddenly change direction, as other, more important thoughts had come into his mind.

But the stories were there to be teased from the mass of words, to be questioned and enlarged. The skeletons that lurked in John's pages had to be given the flesh and blood of reality, even if the dealings and life-style of such character are incredulous to the FLATTY, an ordinary person in the Gypsy vernacular.

The language of the Romany, known as Cant, permeates John's stories, for just as a countryman relaxes into a native dialect, a true Romany finds it difficult to converse without resorting to what, after all, is their native tongue. The stories that are told are John's; many of them were passed on to him by his Romany parents and grandparents; others have evolved from his dealings with people, for in the Cumbrian vernacular, "There's nowt sae queer as folk."

I am assured that all the stories are true, yet no names will disclose the identity of any of those that were involved in deals. Some of the names that are used are those of old time Gypsies, long since gone, no longer able to hear the tales. At John's request, members of his own family are not mentioned by name. *"Some of them have become, what they consider to be respectable people. So don't write their names. We'll just call them The Family."*

Chapter one

THE LOWTHER CONNECTION

John Townsley claims to have family links with the well known Cumbrian family of Lowther, who still own extensive estates in the county. In practically every Cumbrian town, there is to be found a Lowther Street, the name of which acts as a reminder of this once powerful family, who controlled the destiny of a labour force of thousands.

John bases his Lowther connection through his mother, whose maiden name was Ellen Lowther. She was born in Whitehaven, and spent her early years in the West Cumbrian towns of both Whitehaven and Workington. Two prominent branches of the Lowther family are connected with the old county of Cumberland; the west coast Lowthers became powerful through the development of the coal mining industry, while the eastern branch benefited from acquisition of fell and farm land. According to John Townsley's own research, much of this land that was annexed to the Lowther estates was as a result of the Enclosure Acts passed by Parliament between 1780 and 1820.

John Townsley described the Enclosure Acts as *"One of the biggest land grabs in the history of mankind."* He explained, *"Before then it was common land. As the name implies, this was land held by, and for the common people. They used the common land to cut turf, to graze a cow or a sheep, to gather wood for fires or for building, and if they wanted to sow a patch of grain, then they could. There was thousands held these commoners rights."*

The Agricultural Revolution stimulated the Enclosure Acts, as new farming technology and the higher food prices that were brought about as a result of the Napoleonic wars, dictated a more efficient use of land. One statement of the Act of Enclosure said, "That the said commons and waste lands in their present state are incapable of any improvement, and it would be greatly to the advantage of the several persons interested, therein if they were divided to the persons interested."

This implied that the interested persons had to assert their rights in order to register their claim. *"You had to assert your rights, and some of the commoners had forgotten their rights ever existed. So after the Enclosure Acts, their rights disappeared. Fences and hedges went up to enclose the land, and that was the end to the freedom of the commons."*

Many of the seemingly endless miles of dry stone wall that still divide the Lake District today, and separate the "intake" land from the open fell sides, date from the years of the Enclosure Acts when bands of itinerant wallers travelled through the area seeking work.

Some of the more powerful, and knowledgeable families interpreted the enclo-

Tales of a Lakeland Gypsy

sure acts as an opportunity to acquire extra land to add to their own estates. *"There were two main methods by which land could be enclosed, either by private agreement between the landowners involved, or by Act of Parliament. Most of the Lakeland stone walls were built by Act of Parliament following the Enclosure Act of 1801 : under this legislation, the common rights were extinguished, and the land reapportioned among the promoters of the legislation and the holders of rights on the old commons. Not everyone benefited from such changes; thousands of small farmers lost rights of pasturage on the common land and many became mere farm labourers, some paupers."* [Rollinson; Life and Tradition in the Lake District]. The major Cumbrian families of the time were the Senhouses, the Curwens and the Lowthers; they were among those who benefited from the Enclosure Acts.

In John Townsley's opinion, which is based on his own investigation into his family background, some members of the major land owning Lowther families may also trace their roots back to the time when their own forebears were travelling people. John claims his descent from the same stock as the aristocratic branch of the Lowther family on the documentary evidence of his ancestors, as well as family likenesses that recur in succeeding generations. *"Some Lowthers who still live in the county have sons and daughters who are the spitting image of the Lordy's family. Some of the girls have the same hair, teeth and mouth formation, and same facial features. When the Elders decided to settle down, they chose West Cumberland because it had everything. There were coal and iron ore mines; iron works, shipyards and harbours; local fish on the doorstep; quarries and farms, and poachers for salmon. There were railway stations, and horse fairs and plenty of people that were all good for business."*

John's grandfather was Chucky Bob Lowther, who was a legend among travelling folk. *"He was known far and wide as a wily shrewd man who always had the best of driving horses and tackle. He always had a great turnout, whether it was flat carts, gigs or traps. He allus had the best."*

Chucky Bob was a master in dealing. He would dabble in everything that had a potential sale value that was likely to bring in a decent profit. His grandson John described Chucky Bob Lowther as a wide man. *"He was always on the look out for a "mug", especially if he could find him in a pub."* Chucky Bob would go in for a drink, and strike up a conversation with some of the men already there. He was a sociable, friendly character, who attracted attention with his good humoured company and invariably he soon had a crowd gathered round to listen to his tales. *"Are you gonna have a drink with us?"* Chucky Bob would ask. In this way, an unwary onlooker would be drawn into Chucky Bob's circle, enticed by his own curiosity in much the same way as the antics of a gyrating stoat mesmerise an unsuspecting rabbit.

"Once Chucky Bob had drawn him in, he'd got him then, he would be shoved to the bar every time." John explained. The drinking would carry on, with the unsuspecting, "FLATTY" so bemused by alcohol, that he was unaware that it was his money that was actually financing the drinking session of Chucky Bob and his cronies.

Chucky Bob always carried a bag of gold sovereigns and half sovereigns with him, but not all of the coins were what they appeared to be. Some of them were dodgy.

Tales of a Lakeland Gypsy

"They used to make metal coins in a workshop, and then dip them in molten gold." The thin veneer, added to the natural weight of the base metal was sufficient to fool many a person. *"They were what's known as "dipped"* John said, *"It still goes on today over in Istanbul; you can get Queen Victorias, the lot. You can get any bloody reign that you want over in Istanbul. They call them schneides counterfeits."* Gold in all its forms, was and still is, prized by Gypsies. Chucky Bob was a master in passing off these moulded designs of base metal that had been given a fragile coating of gold, that looked like the real thing. *"He would often buy things from drunks and pay them in duds"*, explained John.

In stature, Chucky Bob was a tall, well built man with a great sense of presence that commanded immediate attention in any company. When he was dressed in his fine clothes, he was easily mistaken for a country gentleman. His clothes, like many of his other belongings, often came as a result of craftiness, and getting the better of some "FLATTY".

One of Chucky Bob's favourite tricks was to go into a pub, dressed in scruffy, ragged clothes, and by the force of his personality and bonhomie, encourage a well dressed "FLATTY" to drink with him till the money ran out. Amazingly, and inevitably, Chucky Bob would always discover a half sovereign that had escaped from a torn pocket into the darkness of a jacket lining. With much thought and consideration, he then offered the coin to his drinking partner, in exchange for the clothes off his back.

Befuddled by drink, but charmed and persuaded by his newly found friend, the "FLATTY", accompanied by Chucky Bob, retreated to the back of the pub, where they exchanged their clothes. Chucky Bob, freshly attired in a smart set of country tweeds, and accompanied by the rag clad FLATTY, returned to the bar to drink off the man's freshly acquired half sovereign.

Chucky Bob was a man who would do anything for a bet, and he made a lot of money in this way, visiting pubs as he travelled the county, and throwing down a challenge in those where he was unknown. *"He would go in a pub that was packed out with folk. He would take his Bedlington terrier with him. They're silky blue with long floppy ears,"* John recalled. Chucky Bob had the character and voice to make himself heard above the clamour of a well packed bar. He would shout above all the noise, *"I bet I can nail this dog til a plank o' wood wid two six inch nails, and it'll nivver whimper."* Such an outrageous suggestion immediately brought the room to a hush, and achieved the attention that Chucky Bob was seeking. Such a statement was greeted with the certainty that it couldn't be done, but the packed bar of men didn't know Chucky Bob.

The bets were eagerly placed. *"He took bets in sovereigns with ivverybody in the pub,"* said John as he described how Chucky Bob carried out his claim and nailed his dog to a plank with two six inch nails. Sure enough, and much to the astonishment and dismay of the onlookers, the dog never whimpered. Chucky Bob gleefully pocketed his winnings and went on his way to find other pickings.

John explained how his grandfather had won his bet. *"He didn't put the nails through a leg or part of its body. He laid the dog down and fastened the nails through its big flappin' ears and it nivver even whimpered."*

Chucky Bob was known for pulling strokes in PEEVERS [pubs]. He would pretend to be drunk in order to lead the flatties into thinking they could win a bet off him. With great good humour, and blurred speech, Chucky Bob would flash his gold watch, or sovereigns before the eyes of his prey, lulling the unsuspecting flatties into a false sense of security. He would bet on anything, horses, knuckle fights, or cock fights, but invariably, Chucky Bob came out the winner.

Chucky Bob would challenge any body to a horse race, either on horseback or in a gig or trap. He dealt in horses, and was a sound judge of what an animal could do. In his dealings with the many animals that passed through his hands, he always made sure that he kept the very best. As he had either supplied the horses to many a farmer or countryman that took up his challenge, or had had dealings with them on some occasion, Chucky Bob also knew what their horses could do.

News of a horse race spread like wildfire among the country folk who were always ready for some excitement. A favourite spot to meet was on Winscales Moor, just outside Workington. In addition to the country folk, these races drew townspeople to the scene, many of whom were alert to the chance to make a few shillings on a side bet.

"He was allus on the ball. He lived off his wits. Sometimes he would let on he was running a new horse that he didn't know much about, and at last minute, he'd switch it til a good un that looked exactly the same. Chucky Bob would win. He allus won."

Chucky Bob's judgement of horses was inherited through the family tradition of handling, and selling the animals that were acquired through fair means or foul. Some were legitimately bought, others were taken, or repossessed in settlement of family debts, while some came into their hands as a result of participating in the many raids on outlying farms that went on through the Border area. Sometimes too, the Lowthers were victims of these raids themselves, for on one occasion when they were taking horses to the traditional Gypsy gathering at Appleby, an attempt was made to steal their horses that were paddocked in a farmer's field for an overnight stay. The attempt was foiled however and the Lowthers were able to continue to the horse sale the following day.

In the 18th century, smuggling was rife along the Cumbrian coast. There was no duty on spirits imported into the Isle of Man, and it was a relatively short sea crossing to the Cumbrian coast where teams of pack horses and their handlers were waiting to load up with the contraband of spirits, tobacco, and other goods for distribution to the inland towns. Chucky Bob's forebears were among those who supplied the pack animals to the smugglers.

"They supplied the smugglers with horses and pack mules for transporting merchandise that had come into the local ports. A lot of contraband came into Harrington harbour on small boats, and was also dropped off along the shore line. They took it over the high mountain passes to markets and fairs in various places."

Although he had a settled home in West Cumberland, Chucky Bob was always on the move around the county, for his betting and dealing. He was ever on the lookout for a "mug" that would give him easy pickings, for he was not a man who was fond of work, in the accepted sense of the word. According to the Family, he was a workshy man, who killed his own wife with hard work.

"My grandmother died of hard graft. She was the bread winner and he was a loafer. She used to do all the hawking. She used to drive from Whitehaven all the way to Allonby where there used to be a lot of fishermens' cottages. She would buy the herring there, and sell them on the way back to Whitehaven."

This was round about 1830. When Chucky's wife died at a relatively young age, she left four children to be cared for; there were three girls and one boy. *"Chucky Bob didn't want them,"* said John, *"so he gave them away."* The boy went to Ulverston to live with a wealthy travelling family, and exchanged his Lowther name for that of their family. The three girls, one of whom was John's mother, were brought up by another Romany family, who were related through marriage to Chucky Bob's wife. The Elder, "Old Tom" was regarded by John's mother as *"the finest old gentleman that ever got up of a morning. He was a thorough gentleman."* Old Tom ensured that the girls took no harm. He brought them up as though they were his own children.

This act demonstrates the strength of family feeling that there is among the Romany community. *"If one family is in trouble, another will step in and sort it out, or put them to rights"* said John.

A house in one of the older parts of Cockermouth was a favourite meeting place for travelling people. It was owned by Old Bill Lowther, and as well as being the half way house for those friends and relatives that were on the move, it was always the place for a good crack in Cant. There, the latest happenings among the Gypsy families were discussed, news was brought, and information was shared of deals that had been made or could be made. Old Bill's was also a retreat for any traveller that needed a place to hide out for a few hours before they took to the road again. *"Travellers used to sneak out of Cockermouth in the early hours of the morning with their turn-outs, especially if they had a good MARK. They used to fasten bags round the wheels of the flat carts and traps to deaden the sound. But you could follow the other horse turn-outs on the back roads by the marks left in the soft ground by the iron tyred wheels. If you knew who they were you could BOOL on to catch them up."*

Another Lowther relative, was Andrew Lowther from Keswick. He was cousin to John's mother, and for a time was the world middle weight wrestling champion of the Cumberland and Westmorland style. *"He liked PEEV, [drink], but he used to take part in all the sports like at Grasmere. Andrew Lowther used to hawk herring from a motor bike and side car. He'd tek it all the way up to the farms up on the fell sides in his side car."*

Andrew, with his success and ability in sports was reflecting the tradition of the Lowther family who were well known for their sporting prowess. The most famous among the titled branch of the family was the Lord Lonsdale who was known as "The Yellow Earl". Among the many tales told by travellers about this sporting aristocrat, is how the *"Yellow Earl of Lowther liked nothing better than to go where the Gypsies were camping, and eat with them, and listen to their crack. He would trade lurcher hunting dogs with them."*

John Townsley recalled one tale handed down through his family that concerned a contest between Billy Walsh, a traveller from Darlington, and the Yellow Earl. *"At the hare coursing meetings around Penrith, the Yellow Earl, that was Lordy Lowther used to compete. At one of these meets, Billy Walsh was drawn to meet Lord Lonsdale with his dog. Somehow an argument developed; Lordy accused Billy of getting a flyer, he differed over the slipping of his dog. The Lordy had a sort of quick release attached to the collar of his dog, and the Gypsy man had his silk scarf around the neck of his dog."*

It was alleged that the Yellow Earl accused the Gypsy of stealing a march on him, by slipping his dog too quickly. He wouldn't let the matter drop, and persisted with complaints of illegal slipping so much that Billy challenged the "sporting lord" to a fight. The "Yellow Earl" was well known for his enthusiasm for boxing, for he was the instigator of the "Lonsdale Belts" which are still awarded to British boxing champions. John continued his tale, *"Now Lordy was sort of recognised as being useful with his fists, but he stood no chance against the Gypsy lad, and he was given a real beating that day."*

Another younger, but less prestigious member of the Lowther family also had great sporting success in the horse racing field; this was John Townsley's brother in law, William Lowther.

"William Lowther was much sort after by lots of money people; wealthy farmers, hotel owners, and various business people to ride their horses. He could master misfit horses, and he rode all over the north of England, pulling off some large bets. He rode at York, Cark in Cartmel winning silver cups everywhere. He also won the Dearham Derby and the Ellenborough Gallops. It was sometimes called the Pitmens' Derby, that they used to have in the holiday times in Cumberland. I was just a young boy when I went to this particular race at Ellenborough on a bank holiday Monday. This was the last time they had a meeting at Ellenborough. The owner that Bill was riding for had some good horses; one of them stood out, it was called Nettler."

Nettler had a fine reputation as a winning horse and consequently, as far as the betting was concerned, it only carried short odds when it was entered for a race. To give a better return on his wager, Nettler's owner entered his horse for the race, but under a different name. *"He had changed its name from Nettler to Alf's Button, and he had a lot of money on that horse. It won. The bookmakers never twigged until everybody had gone home, and there was hell to play. But it was too late. At these meetings there was no rules as such, and nothing was done about it."*

William rode in point to point events, steeplechases, flat racing, as well as taking part in the jumping events that were held at county shows. He was a good judge of horses, and brought many pure breds back from Ireland for his special customers. He had a good reputation for being a fair man to deal with.

"People used to congregate on the camping ground on the Cloffocks at Workington; business people, Gypsy people, horsey people, watching him ride and drive and jump

all types of horses he had for sale. He put them through the paces to flash them, and show their full potential. Money used to change hands as deals were struck. It was all cash in those days."

John recalled some of the days when he used to go with Bill to some of the show jumping events in the county. *"He used to use all his knowledge getting jumpers to lift their legs at a jump. He would take a horse he was jumping to a quiet part of the field, and he would tone it up there where it was nice and quiet. He used to use all his knowledge and know how, to get them ready for the jumps. He knew all sorts of ways to get them lift up for the jumps."*

When William attended the shows, he always took saddles, heavy cart gear and driving harnesses to sell. *"He had a wide MUSH [man] doing it for him."* William Lowther also used to travel throughout the county buying in all sorts of wool, or empty cloth sacks that could be sold on to someone else, but always at a profit. While travelling in this way he would often stay out overnight sleeping rough in a barn, or if the weather was fine, he slept in the open air underneath the shelter of his cart. At other times he sold herring and hawked pots and pans in the manner of the rest of the Family.

"I went with him when I had holiday from school, we went all over the fell country. I used to jump out of the cart and open and shut fell gates, and open and shut farm lonning gates leading down to the farms. We used to trade all the time, returning with farm eggs, old hens, sausage or a bit of pig or pork. He used to make it known among the farming folk who he had married, because although he was a Lowther, my sister's name of Townsley meant a lot to country folk."

Little John Lowther was another well respected dealer who was cousin to John's mother, Ellen Lowther. Little John travelled the area between Whitehaven and Millom and dealt with many farmers and business people. *"He bought horses and tackle from us to sell in South Cumberland. He travelled like a country gentleman, buying and selling horses down there in the best turnouts that money could buy. Farmers and business people would never deal with anybody else but Little John Lowther; such was his reputation for fair dealing."*

Dealing, coursing, racing, wrestling were all aspects of the travelling Lowthers' life-style, and Chucky Bob's daughter Ellen was no stranger to the wrestling holds, *"She could throw a cross buttock with the best of them"* her son recalled. There must have been a lot of Chucky Bob's character in Ellen, for she took over the domination of her branch of the Lowther family, and carried it through when she married.

Among the many old Gypsy sayings is the following, *"It's said if it's man or beast and it's got DINGLY CLARET in its breeding, it will come out and throw back for ever."* The genes handed down to John through his mother Ellen may support John's claim to his Lowther connections. They may indeed be well founded, for his own facial features, when compared to those of James Lowther, who was a Member of Parliament from 1840 -1904, show a striking and uncanny resemblance. *"He would often use CANT in his private conversation"* said John

Chapter Two

THE TOWNSLEY FAMILY

The Townsleys, like the Lowthers were of Romany stock, but they originated from Scotland. Some members of the family moved into England in the 1700's, and when times became hard in the early 20th century, a number of them emigrated to Canada. and America, to begin a new life, and there to create a new dynasty. John Townsley explained the work ethos of travelling people. *"Like the true, pure breed of all travellers, they worked for no one, only themselves."*

The Townsleys who settled to live in West Cumberland, as it then was known, had wandered and camped in many different parts of the county, with their horses and wagons for many years, before some of them decided to settle and make a permanent home near Whitehaven.

"In the olden days, some of them used to go camping in the summer. The others would say, Why travel when we have everything we need in West Cumberland? If we are looking for UTOPIA this is the nearest thing we will get to it. They used to say, a rolling stone gathers no more moss."

The Townsleys were horse dealers, and the women folk were mistresses of the hawking trade. They made their own baskets, from which they could sell, and buy almost everything that made "ROWDY" [money].

The essential household equipment that every town and country family needed included pottery of all descriptions, and many of the small West Cumbrian villages during the 18th and 19th century had a pottery that made utensils for local use, as well as selling to traders to carry round the countryside. In Hutchinson's History of Cumbria 1794/7, it is recorded that manufactory at Dearham had " A noted one of coarse pottery". The pottery was also recorded in Bulmer's Directory of Cumberland, 1901. "The Jubilee Pottery was formerly known as the Dearham Pottery where a quantity of brown earthen ware was manufactured."

"I have heard the Elders saying there was a pottery near Dearham and a lot of travellers used to camp there in the summer months. The women used to buy large dishes that could be used for all kinds of things in farmhouses and ordinary houses. The travelling women used to carry them on their heads, and travel round locally selling them to country folk." Carrying goods on the head was commonplace among the travellers. *"I have seen my sisters put baskets full of all kinds of hawking SWAG up on their heads."*

There was a tradition in the Townsley family of fish selling, which they had practised in their native Scotland, so when the West Cumbrian Townsleys gave up their itinerant way of life, they started to buy fish from the local harbours and sell it from their traps in the surrounding country districts. As they became more prosperous

Tales of a Lakeland Gypsy

through their horse trading and hawking businesses, they made their home at Tarn House, Lowca, of which now only a few outline walls remain. The farm was situated about half way between Whitehaven and Workington, and only a few hundred yards away from what was then, the busy port of Harrington.

Their dealings in anything and everything, in addition to the fish trade, brought further prosperity to the Townsley family, and the two sons, Big Charlie as he was known, and John were able to marry and have families of their own. John Townsley married Ellen Lowther, the daughter of Chucky Bob Lowther and they moved to their own home in Harrington, where they settled in the higher part of the village in the old lonnin' which was known as Potters' Lonnin'.

"The two families of Townsleys, their fathers, and those before that for genera-tions, men and women, were masters of the all round business." John recalled. Horse dealing, selling carpets, SWAG of all kinds, fish, poultry, rabbits and game, as well as pots, pans, rubbing stone and tuggery were bought and sold to make every penny work. On a higher level, there were dealings in gold and silver, scrap jewellery and even money lending, to swell the Family coffers. The Family scorned keeping their wealth in commercial banks, and preferred to keep their prized gold sovereigns close to hand.

"My uncle, Big Charlie would go into the Galloping Horse Inn at High Harrington on a Saturday night. It was an old whitewashed place with stables and a big yard. The landlord was an unstable sort of character. He eventually hung himself in the stables. Big Charlie would pull out his draw string bag, and it would be full of gold sovereigns, and he would buy a drink for everybody. My dad would be in with him, but he only drank soda water for his health. Big Charlie would put on a show, letting people know that he was the big wheel. My dad was much quieter, he always played it cool."

It was said of the Townsley brothers, *"when they were both young men, they could run alongside of a horse in harness, jump cleanly over their backs, and back again, whilst the horse was into a fair trot."* Some years later, Ellen Townsley said to her youngest son John, *"I could have had my pick of travelling GADGES, but there was only one for me, and that was your father John Townsley; the best that ever lived. He had some good yokes and horses and other tackle, and a bag of gold sovereigns."*

Big Charlie also married, and his wife was a member of the same family that had taken Ellen into care when her mother died. Both families lived quite close to each other in cottages that were in the Harrington country lane. When the the brothers left their parents home at Tarn House, that lane in Harrington became the centre of the family business. Stables and outhouses, barns and warehouses grew up alongside the row of houses in which members of the families lived. Potters' Lonnin' as it was locally called, was also known as Travellers' Lonnin'.

"Outside, and chained to our house was old canons on iron wheeled carriers, also there was the cannon balls for these weapons. We had horses heads made out of stone on the walls. The houses were full of water colour paintings of country scenes and pictures of trotting horses and harness horses that we had owned. In the yards we kept fighting cocks and bantams, we also had canaries in cages that used to sing as soon

Tales of a Lakeland Gypsy

as the frying pans were put on at breakfast time. We kept guard dogs that were bred to worry. We got them to do this by baiting them, and trying to break their temper. When all the men were away for days on end, the women knew they were safe with the dogs on guard. They ran on long chains in the yards. Country people used to come to us to buy them for guard dogs on their own property."

The growling and barking of these animals as they strained to despatch an unsought for stranger was sufficient protection for the womenfolk and young children while the men were away. But even for the men folk, there was potential danger on the roads. Neither family used banks for their money, all their dealings were made in cash, and it was well known when the families were off dealing and that they carried a ready supply of money with them.

At times like this, they ran the risk of being robbed, especially when they were travelling out of their own area to be among strangers in Scotland, Wales or especially Ireland. Times were hard, and people would do anything, and that included robbery with violence, to get hold of some money. They never knew who they were dealing with, and consequently ensured that they took their own precautions.

"My people always carried loaded whips and a weapon when out on the road, and they were never afraid to use them. They dealt with all kinds of people, some you could say were lawless, and as money was scarce, you didn't need anything else. You could say that was the target, for robbers knew that respectable hawkers, and dealers carried money. The Elders talked about the desperate people they had met on the highway. They always went in numbers for protection, and sometimes took two or three well known fighting men with them in case of trouble. My people carried sovereigns, cash money and Bradbury's; banks were hardly ever used in those days. They liked to carry their cash, or keep their money nearby."

Both the brothers continued to be partners in the horse trading, but each went their own way in the many and varied businesses that sprang up alongside their dealings. *"Everyone of the Families congregated in Big Charlie's house every night to say where they had been that day, and what had happened. So in this way, they all knew what was going on and the MARKS and the deals that were about to be done. My people were in the Whillimoor and Tuet hill country every day; hawking, dealing, selling and buying and I used to go with my Elders from the age of five."*

John recalled that it was all manual work, day in and day out, not only for his family but for the people of the farming communities. *"There was no cars in those days, and the people who did not have a horse and cart had to walk everywhere. They used scythes to cut the hay in the fields, and wheel barrows with old wood across the top, to bring the hay into the old broken down barns. We used to buy home made Whillimoor cheese from the farmers' wives; its name was really "Whillimoor Wang".*

Looking back from the motor crowded streets of the late 20th century, it is difficult to relate to a time when they were busy, not with cars, but with horse drawn vehicles of every description. Deliveries of milk and coal, green groceries and general goods, fish and butcher's meat were all sold from the back of a horse drawn cart. Even the patients that had recovered from an infectious illness at the local isolation hospital

19

were returned to their homes and families, not in the comfort of a well sprung ambulance, but bounced along on the back of a horse drawn cart. The doctor made his rounds in a trap or a gig, the parson did his visits on horseback or in his trap, and this was also the only way in which people were able to visit other parts of the county; unless they were prepared to walk. There were no buses, steam trains were in their infancy, and the motor car was a mere dream on a distant horizon. The farmers relied on the heavy horses for working their land, and delivery merchants needed horses to pull their carts. People needed horses for their every day lives and the Townsleys were the men to supply them.

The Townsley brothers were always on the look out for the finest animals that they could buy cheaply and sell at a profit. In those days, having a good horse and turnout was like the status symbol of the modern day motor car. Business people and gentry saw their horses and carriages as an advertisement for their standing in the commercial world, or to declare their status in the hierarchy of a country community *"My family did a lot of horse dealing with wealthy folk."* said John.

In the days before the Great War, the Townsley brothers travelled to Ireland and Wales to buy horses. Welsh cobs were much sought after for carriage horses, while the Irish horses could be obtained quite cheaply. *"They went to Ireland and Wales to buy their horses. They would land them by boat into Glasgow, and drive them loose with a turnout in front and one behind. They would stop at farmhouses and drive into the farm yards, or a nearby paddock and stay there for the night. They would sleep either in a barn or under the traps, or a flat cart. At the break of day, they would be up and away. They always carried pistols and lead loaded sticks, and perhaps they would have a couple of fighting men for protection."*

Many of the Welsh horses were driven north to a Lancashire port where they were loaded on to a boat for the journey to be completed by sea.

"These horses would be sold at home, or at the horse fairs. They always had some customers waiting for new driving and riding horses."

There was an old farmer at Distington, who always liked the best of driving horses. He travelled to auction markets all over the county, where he met up with other farmer friends and enjoyed a "drop of drink", during the day's business. He owned a fine, black driving horse that was the talk of the district, and was greatly admired by anyone that knew anything about horses. The old man also fancied himself as a bit of a dealer, and went to Cockermouth Auction every week.

The two Townsley brothers were among those who fancied the old farmer's black driving horse, and set up a plan "to lift it" when the old man was returning from the local auction. Monday is still the traditional day for Cockermouth Auction, when farmers from all over the district bring their sheep and cattle to be traded off. So it was on a late Monday afternoon that the Townsley brothers lay in wait for the old farmer driving his horse back home.

"They were laying in wait for Jack on his way home. They were on top of Winscales Moor. They pulled him up for a crack and in the end, challenged him to a race from

Tales of a Lakeland Gypsy

Crossbarrow to his stable in Distington for any money. Jack said he would trot them for horse against horse, and that was the wager.

They shook hands with him. They beat him home by a fair distance, and when he came, they took the black horse out of his trap. That was theirs. It was said that it was some horse, this black cob, but the old "gadgie" didn't know how to get the best out of it, and get it to perform on its top note."

Trading in, and acquiring horses by any means, fair or foul was not the only line of business that the Townsley's successfully pursued, for they were both involved in the same sort of fish dealing business as had been practised by Chucky Bob's wife. Whereas she collected her herring and kippers from the seaside village of Allonby, the Townsley brothers obtained their supply from Parton, which was much nearer to their home. Herrings from Parton were renowned throughout the county. They had a reputation for being of the finest quality that was caught in the Solway.

Charlie and John Townsley used to load their carts up in the early summer evenings with the herring and other fish that were brought in by the small boats that beached along the West Cumbrian coast. *"They made their way overnight through Gosforth, and over the high mountain roads to Ambleside, Windermere and on to Kendal"*, said John and added that his dad and uncle took the opportunity to sell fish to farms that they passed on the way. When the Townsley brothers went out travelling with their fish, they also took other goods such as pots and pans, rugs and blankets, as it was never known what the country folk would need. They also travelled with a number of horses tied up behind their carts for there was always someone in the country that was in need of a fresh animal for riding or pulling a trap. While they were out in the country selling their fish, they were also on the look out for contacts with poachers or farmers who were able to supply them with salmon or sea trout that migrated into rivers and becks on their land, These were bought and brought back with them to sell to hotels that they passed on their return journey home.

"They used to say the Townsleys came into a village at the end of the day with a few herring they had left out of a load. The empty herring boxes would be filled with salmon and trout caught by country people and poachers. One old man said the Townsleys came into the village and took out more fish than they brought in. When the salmon and trout season was in, we had transport that picked the fish up on our rounds. We used to leave the pick up points to last thing of the day. Farmers also sold us fish that passed through the rivers on their land. We also bought from game keepers and water bailiffs who worked for a pittance in those days; they badly needed the money to live a little better."

"We bought fish that came out of all the local rivers, the Derwent, Ellen. the Cocker, the Calder, the Marron and all their tributaries. We supplied hotels in different parts of Cumberland and Lancashire, and other northern counties; we delivered them by rail to different parts of the country. We also got beautiful trout out of the river Liza that comes down past Pillar Rock into Ennerdale lake. The poachers used to net the river there, where it enters the lake, and sometimes they used night lines."

One of the largest salmon that the Townsleys bought was one that was reputed to weigh 72 pounds, and was taken out of the river Derwent near Camerton. There is no actual record of the weight of this monster, for it was not caught legally on a rod and line. It was bought from a well known local family of poachers and John Townsley explained, *"the weight was such that it had to be weighed on a local farmer's potato scales."* The fish was so long that when the Townsley's carried it away on their fish cart, it's tail hung over the end!

One of the many buildings in the lane where the Family lived always used to be left open at night for the local salmon poachers, who came to drop off their catch. *"Poaching wasn't looked on as a big deal then; it was just something that towny and country folk did to make a bit of extra money."* One of the Family would be inside waiting for them to come. There was always a big fire awaiting them, for the poachers were often wet through. Warmed outside by the fire, and inside by a welcome drink, the poachers collected the ready money for their night's work. Poachers were not the only visitors who came down the lane late at night, for as well as those who came to give tip offs about unwanted animals that were going cheap, or where there was some scrap to be lifted, there were the more innocent wanderers who dropped in for a meal and a sing song round the fire.

"Both families used to like to hear good CHANTERS, [singers], accordion and melodeon players; the tin whistlers and the Irish singers. Sometimes dealers came who were clog dancers, and that was their only pleasure, and entertainment. They used to get round the fire in one of the houses and talk." The main topic of conversation was of course, horses. *"That was their main pleasure to talk about the good goers they had had, and where there was one they would like to get hold of. They knew all the HALF WIDE men who would call on them to let them know what was doing and who was sick of an animal. Perhaps they knew of any COLD SHOULDERED ones or any other MISFITS."*

An open table was always kept for those who came to do business with the Townsleys. One old dealer recorded the hospitality he had received, *"We always knew we would be well fed when we called, cold winter evenings after having a deal. Before setting off for home, we were given a hot meal and the best of food before the road home."* Others that took advantage of the Townsley hospitality were the cattle drovers, who used to drive their charges of both cattle and horses over long distances to deliver them to or from market. *"We used to let the cattle drovers sleep in our stables when they couldn't get home at night. There were lots of them throughout the north, and many were well known to the family as they attended all the sales."*

The years that followed the end of the first world war brought hard times for the folks who lived in West Cumberland. *"Money was tight in those days, but my dad always had plenty of things to sell to people. The women at home used to make home made jams like rhubarb and ginger, blackberry and blackcurrant. They would pickle onions, red cabbage and beetroots. In autumn at the weekends, the men would go into the woods and gather bags full of hazel-nuts."* Although much of this food for free was kept for their own use, there was always plenty to sell from the carts along with the pots and pans, items of drapery, and TUGGERY, [old clothes]. Sometimes, the things that were sold were on CHUCKY, [credit] and on occasions, there was difficulty in getting the money that was due; but a debt was never forgotten. John Townsley recalled how his father and Big Charlie had been CHUCKED by an old Cockermouth man who dealt in horses. He had bought coal off the brothers during one of the coal strikes, when they sold coal gathered from the shore, and dug from local out crops.

"When my Uncle Charlie drove through to Cockermouth on market days to get the money off a certain man, his friends used to say, he has gone home, he is a real bad fettle. When he got to know that the Townsleys were in town and were looking for him, he would hide in different people's houses till they had gone. In the end, they just went to his stables and took horses and tackle that was equivalent to what they were owed, and their loss of time coming to be paid. Nobody offered any resistance because the families were well known for taking people on when they were owed money."

This was a lesson that young John Townsley learned early in his life; a debt owed had to be paid, even if some considerable time elapsed.

"I was but a boy, and I had been with one of the cousins delivering two horses we had sold to a farmer. It was late in the day when we were making for home, when around a bend in this narrow country road there was a man with a horse and spring cart. We pulled into the middle of the cart track and stopped him. My cousin jumped down off the trap and said, You are the man we have been looking for for a few months, and I believe you have moved.

He said, Yes, I live 12 or 13 miles away from where I lived with my mother.

You have never paid for the goods you got off our lasses; and you promised you would. So for what you and your family owe us altogether, I am taking your turnout.

How will I get home? he asked.

Like everybody else; you'll have to walk, and thank your lucky stars that I have not set about you."

John was told to drive their turnout while his cousin drove back the one he had taken in settlement of the debt. *"We never heard any more about it. This man owed the girls money, and he had to pay."*

The brothers would sell anything that would raise money and they were prepared to get up early in the morning to get the carts loaded ready for the road. *"Yes there was always a lot of action down our lane. My father used to be up watering and feeding livestock around four thirty to five o clock in the morning. The women would be up every morning around five o clock to make the breakfasts ready then down to the station to meet the fish train. Then the fish had to be brought back and sorted out for each individual turnout. Then there would be a stampede to hit the road for a good start. They used to say that one hour in the morning was worth two in the afternoon.*

There would be anything up to ten turnouts leaving the lane every morning. Some were with fish or herring to go round different areas of countryside, selling a lot on CHUCKY, to get money at the weekend, or some went round hawking pots or china in a Kendal pot cart. They had raised sides with the tops spindled, and variegated to break their plainess. They were shaped like a canoe so that the pots were safe, packed

23

Tales of a Lakeland Gypsy

in straw for the journeys down the rough country lanes."

Some of the turnouts or carts would set off empty, as their drivers went on the look out for scrap metal, rabbit skins, sheeps' wool, or anything that people wanted to sell. *"They bought all kinds of pelts and various skins off the gamekeepers, farmers and butchers. They always kept them for my father and his brother. Many times they used to come out of the country with their carts loaded up with all sorts of animal skins. Fox skins, mole skins, stoats, weasels, hair pelts, all the game keepers on the large estates kept them for us. We dried and stretched them on the hundreds of nails that were in the oak beams in a drying room. They were hung up to dry in the skin sheds that were well away from the houses, and were then baled up and sent by rail to the skin factories."*

John Townsley junior could remember rabbits and pheasants being bought from farmers at 6d a time. *"We paid 6d for rabbits and a similar price for pheasants, partridge and hares. When we sold them to customers in the town, we always skinned them, so we got profit on the rabbit or hare, and the skins that were sent away to the skin factory."* The feathers of the partridges and pheasant were also turned to profit. *"We also bought wild bird feathers, and sometimes full wings of birds, as well as feather beds. Lots of feathers went to the hat makers, and sometimes they would ask us to get any special feathers that they wanted."*

The women and the girls of the Family had the job of skinning the rabbits, and filleting the fish; the latter was especially a cold, unpleasant job in hard weather when the chill of the air, combined with the iciness of the fish to render hands chapped and red.

Ellen Townsley, wife of John senior, was not overshadowed by her husband's many deals, for she went on to become one of the shrewdest dealers of them all. It was reputed that she could often make the deal where many of the men folk had failed. *"In the early 1900's my mother was heading into the "high country" with a good turnout and she met her nephew, young Tom Townsley, a boy of fifteen summers. He told her, I called on a farmer who has just bought two good galloways [horses]. I tried to buy them off him but I could not manage, but I know that you are well got with him and his wife and you could lift them."*

Ellen immediately headed for the farm where the two galloways were to be found. She went to the stables to have a look at the animals knowing that the farmer was a man who always liked a deal. She started to bid him for these two driving horses. *"In the end she buys them. Some ROWDY down, and the rest CHUCKY. She tied them up behind her turnout and lands them up down our travellers lonnin".*

At the start of the 1914 world war, John Townsley senior was employed to work on the railways. *"He drove the engines on the local lines drawing loaded goods wagons from the steel works and arms factories, so the job was all right for CHOREY, and there was always a good supply of BLACKIES or YAGS for the KENS. The railway ran within a stones throw from our yards and houses."*

It's not difficult to imagine that some of the metal that was being carried in the goods wagons was diverted to the nearby family yards, and there absorbed into the goods that John Townsley senior bought legitimately from wholesalers and warehouses.

"He had been buying all kinds of goods from a firm down country, getting them delivered in box vans to the station at High Harrington. He had van loads of goods that he supplied to shops as well as for hawking them round himself. He would send a sum of money, in cash, ROWDY, to this firm every now and again. But for several box van consignments, they tried to come it by saying they had not received the cash, even though my dad had paid receipts. They didn't seem to be interested; someone had been pocketing the money.

But the time came when it got harder to sell, as every one had been supplied over and over again, and money was scarce. This firm said my dad owed quite a lot of money so they sent the bailiffs in, with the law to take anything that he owned which was saleable. They couldn't take the house or the yard because it was owned by my mother, so they said they would take the flat carts, the gigs, the traps and about twelve or fourteen horses that were tied up in the stables, and of course, he always had a bag of sovereigns and bank notes stashed away in his brother's house in the lane."

All the horse tackle that the bailiffs had their eye on was owned by John in partnership with his brother Big Charlie. With the uproar and argument that arose in the lane it wasn't long before there was a supportive response from the other members of the Townsley family. Seven strapping, fit young men who were all over six feet tall, emerged to confront the bailiff and his two henchmen. One of them stepped forward.

"Up stepped a young man, Charlie's eldest son, who was also called John. He was the brainy one of the family. He said I am John Townsley; that man is my uncle and he owns nothing but a house full of kids that he can't feed. The carts, the horses, the harnesses are mine, I have it in writing, so you had best be on your way."

The atmosphere of barking guard dogs, and the gathering numbers of an irate family were not an encouragement for the bailiffs to stay *"and they departed empty handed. Someone said you are one for another you Townsleys, and one of them said, we **are** one for another."*

There were other brushes with the law. *"There used to be a police inspector in Harrington eighty or ninety years ago called Bone. He arrived down our lane one day when everyone was away doing business, but my mother was in.*

What would you be wanting today Inspector?

Your husband, if he's around.

If you walk down Scaw road to where it joins the Winscales road, you will meet him coming, Ellen told the Inspector.

Cheerio, he said, and away he went swinging his stick."

Ellen watched him until he was out of sight and then immediately called all the younger members of both families, that had not gone out on the rounds, to come quickly.

Tales of a Lakeland Gypsy

"She used to use a large basket for carrying clothes to dry out on the hedge in the field. She loaded the basket up several times with the DUKE [metals]. Together, they all moved the CHOREY metals into the nearby field and dropped them into a small ghyll, where they covered the metal over with branches and leaves. While this was going on, one of the Family kept look out on the road.

A good time later, my dad came flying into the yard with his turnout and the police inspector was riding with him. She gave the men a sign that everything was CUSHTY.

Both men got down from the cart and the inspector looked round the yard and in the sheds, under sheets and behind carts, looking for anything that should not have illegally been there. But he was too late when he looked round; the bird had flown."

After the end of the first world war, the Townsleys began to use mechanised transport for some of their rounds, although horses remained their main line of business for many years. *"One of my older cousins was Charlie Townsley. He had been into horses for many years but after the first world war, he was into cars like bull nosed Morris and Lagondas. Cousin Charlie could make money while other people slept. He sold salmon to hotels throughout the Lake District, and he was also into supplying rugs and carpets far and near."*

It was with another cousin, and his Uncle Big Charlie, that John had his early experiences of travelling the high country by mechanised transport. *"I used to go with them hawking with a Lagonda in the lakes, selling rugs, and PONGO [linoleum], they were also dealing in gold time pieces; buying and selling them, and asking about other things at the same time, such as horses, carts, harness and lamps. I didn't see any other Gypsies around at those times; we more or less had the area to ourselves to go hawking. With using the Lagonda, or a bull nosed Morris, we could get further out into the area, and come back home each night. Petrol was cheap, and you got it at small shops in the country in two gallon tins. Sometimes we had a couple of tins of petrol strapped to the running board in a proper made stand."* John Townsley explained that his dad used to buy lots of metals from quarry and colliery bosses, *"and although the metals were probably not gotten just quite right, he wasn't going to give them away."*

Another dodge that the Family had for acquiring and hiding doubtful material was by using the body of an old model T Ford lorry. *"It had a false body, and a box fastened underneath, and a trap door. It was used for collecting CHOREY from various works, and it was also used for buying and selling over the weigh bridge. Into it would be put cast iron blocks when touching for weight. After it had been weighed, these were taken out after it was weighed empty. They were put in again when delivering to local works or mills, or failing that, the man working the weigh bridge would be squared. It was searched time and time again, but its secret was never discovered."*

If life seemed to be all hard work for the Families, then there was the compensation of idyllic summer evenings when they would all gather in the lane under the hawthorn hedge and talk over the days events. Part of the hedge had been clipped to form a green and living settee, and there the Elders would wait for some of the younger members of the family who were late back from the "high country"; but although they were relaxing, they were never idle. The good humoured chat and banter accompanied the

26

Tales of a Lakeland Gypsy

jobs that could be done in the communal atmosphere of the Family.

"They used to sit and wait for the latecomers coming back. They used to talk there at the gathering place during the long summer nights. Some would be sitting cleaning harness, eating hazel nuts gathered in the woods. The women folk gathered together, some would be making new mats and hearth rugs and others would be knitting."

These communal Family gatherings carried on throughout the long, dark nights of winter, but instead of the welcome shade from a hawthorn hedge, they took place closed round the cheerful warmth of a fire blazing indoors. *"They talked about the countryside they had been in that day and who they had seen on their rounds, and what deals they had pulled off that day. My brother Charlie rarely left Workington when he was selling fish because he was known in every street."*

There was a close relationship between the young Townsley cousins, who were more like brothers, for wherever one went, they all went. John Townsley, being the youngest boy was not old enough to join his brother and cousins in their sometimes questionable activities, but remembers that they got into some scrapes. *"The cousins were wide awake operators. Tom was the most daring. Black blue curly hair, six foot three inches tall, he was a very good looking young man, and he was always up to some caper. He could spot a MARK a mile away. Charlie and Jamesey were dead wide young men, and were good at any job. They all moved together and all three were part of the action. Then the MUSKERS would come down the lane.*

Hello Inspector, the young ones would say. Are you wanting someone?

Are the three boys around?

No, they are out with their turnouts earning a living; what did you want them for?

Just that they had been up to their skylarking down town.

They were always looking and asking for information about CHOREY, and who was camping here and there with anything to deal."

John Townsley Junior recalled that his father never had the best of health. *"He was always on the move, out in all sorts of weathers, turning his hands to buying and selling anything."* In 1926, his father became seriously ill, and his wife Ellen summoned her eldest son, Charlie, to come home from Canada, where he had emigrated a number of years earlier. When Charlie returned, he naturally assumed the position as head of his family's business. He settled down to his former lifestyle, and soon adapted into the old routine as if he had never been away. He was into buying and selling, trucking and trading in and around the town of Workington along with the rest of the Family. But events were to prove that it was not a happy home coming, even though he carried out a lot of business in Workington, and people were pleased to see him back. His father's illness continued, and his condition became progressively worse. Shortly after Charlie returned from Canada, his father John died at the age of 46.

For a while Charlie carried on with the business. *"One day, he came home after being away in the "High Country", his cart was loaded up with old goods he had bought and tied to the cart were two newly bought horses. He complained of being real bad fettle, and went to bed. We got the doctor, but Charlie never got up again. He died*

27

of pneumonia six months after the death of his father. That was a real blow to the family, and my mother blamed herself for bringing him back from Canada."

Ellen Townsley was filled with remorse on the death of her son, feeling that by bringing him back from Canada, she was responsible for his death; but the business had to go on. It was as well that Ellen Townsley was adept at dealing, for following the death of both her husband and her eldest son dead, she then had to take over the responsibility of carrying on the family business, with the help of her six daughters, and surviving son, John.

There was no widow's pension, no income support, no child allowance or any of the modern day benefits to claim to ease the financial burden. Her husband had managed his own business without contributing to any pension scheme, but he made sure that Ellen was not left penniless. *"She was left with good tackle, and horses and carts, and a bag of gold sovereigns. The older end of the Family had had a good grounding in the business, and they knew how to carry on."*

A young John Townsley on horseback down Potters' Lonnin'

Mother Ellen with John's sister Nellie

Chapter Three

MOTHER ELLEN

After the deaths of both her husband and eldest son, Ellen Townsley was left with the task of keeping the rest of her family together. The business was safe in her capable hands, but they all had to share the work to ensure they were able to keep it going.

"She was an all round traveller, and could hawk, sell and buy horses. Also she had a way with her which must have been handed down, or it could have been a gift. She could open any doors. By that, I mean she was clever and smart. She could spot a mug or a mark a hundred yards away. She had learned her business off her father, Chucky Bob. She knew the area backwards."

Ellen Townsley was known to other travellers as a sharp, clever woman, and although she was unable to read or write, and could only sign for her own name with a cross, it was unheard of for anyone to outwit her in a deal. A Romany woman recalled her parents talking about Ellen. "My mam and dad used to say Ellen Townsley could do the business, and had a way with her that was rather special. She was always looking out, and was alert for MARKS, and pulling them off. She always carried a money bag in the pocket of her clothes ready to buy anything. Even though she couldn't read and write, it was no handicap to her. She was a real character, and very clever with it; a master at dealing and talking."

Ellen Townsley was born in 1864, and in spite of her own disturbed childhood when she was rejected by her father after her mother died, she grew up to be a good humoured person, with a strong sense of right and wrong as far as the Family was concerned. In appearance she was tall and strong, and would stand no nonsense either from her own children, or from any of the men or women with whom she was dealing. *"She always stood up to dealing men, and never backed off."* She was strong enough and able enough to "cross buttock" any man. Yet, she was a calm natured woman and usually nothing ever bothered her. She was described by many as a woman and a half, but could be, in the words of her son, *"a real ball of fire"* when roused.

"When there was anyone, man or woman who had to be approached to be spoken to, for a straightener to be put up to them, or to do a deal when others had failed, Ellen Townsley was the one to do it. She was the master, and had a way which must have been given by God to gain people's confidence, if she had to touch for BUNCE, or to draw things on the side."

It was said of Ellen Townsley that she could spot a RAFFIE a mile away, be it a MANISHER or a GADGIE and she could work on anyone who she smelled was something else. She never went to school, for being Chucky Bob Lowther's daughter, it was work in the family tradition that was important, not schooling. Everything that

30

was done in the way of business had to be right and correct, and also the house and the turnouts had to be kept in spotless condition. When her husband and eldest son died, Mother Ellen made sure that her six daughters and one surviving son continued with the grounding in the business that had been begun by their father. *"What a family. We were all alert and did the job we were told to do every day. There was no arguing or falling out. We knew the Family way of life and were adept at carrying it out. We knew the FLATTY ANTLE from year in and year out, and the best way to exploit the FLATTY. The GOUGER people, if they had a job in the in the early 1900's thought they were better FLATTY than us. Maybe they went to work on an old bike, or walked it. We had our yokes and our carts. But they would CHUCKY from us a bit till the weekends. Sometimes they would say. They are just potters from down the Potters Lonnin', but we did own it and had bags of sovereigns and a box of white Bradbury notes upstairs.*

My sisters were the best. They all were educated and schooled to know what was what, and right from wrong. They never gave my mother one minute of anxiety. They had been shown the game of hawking and buying and selling by the shrewdest traveller there was; my mother. They worked from sun up to sun set, and did everything that was asked of them. Rich or poor, it didn't matter who they dealt with; their word was their bond. Big KENS, [homes] BARRY ANTLE [ordinary folk] it was all the same to them. They just simply knew their job."

For the girls, it was work all the time. Sleep was their only respite. There was no radio, no television to distract their attention from the jobs in hand. They had to make their own pleasure with what little time they had available. Each member of the family had their own job to do. One daughter, Nellie, organised the ordering of goods and the paying of bills, and generally looked after the business side of things. Each of the other sisters had their own rounds with the horses and carts that took goods into parts of the nearby towns, or ventured further afield into what they called "the high country", that area on the western fringe of Lakeland where the low fell lands merge with the coastal plain of the Cumbrian coast. There were many hamlets and villages; scattered farms and cottages that were visited by different members of the Family on a regular basis.

Each day of the week saw all the members of the family astir by five o' clock. Some would prepare the breakfast, while others attended to the horses and turnouts. Even the canary would start its first song of the day as the porridge was being stirred in the huge iron pan. No member of the family was allowed to to take their breakfast until the horses had been seen to. The horses were the family's life line, they had to be kept in the best of condition and be fit to take the carts on to the road each day and every day. *"Weekends was as busy as any other day. Collecting CHUCKY [money], selling game and old TUGGERY [clothes], it was a never ending circle."*

The girls that were going out with their traps always had an early, but hearty breakfast of porridge, FONKY ham, which always hung upon hooks in the cellar, fried bread, plenty of strong tea and heaps of toast. While they were eating the meal that would sustain them for most of the day, other members of the Family would check and load up the carts. They would eat later once the carts were ready for the road. Lizzie Townsley used to travel every day to the country areas to the east of Harrington

Tales of a Lakeland Gypsy

following a route that visited such villages as Ennerdale, Frizington and Branthwaite, while some of her other sisters would work the villages nearer to home.

"The farmers used to stop their work in the fields to watch the girls pass by in their traps. So regular were they on their routes, that many a farm worker would gauge the time of day by the hour that they passed him by. The farming people would watch my sisters driving the turnouts, and marvelled at how they handled those horses."

John Townsley recalled that his sister Lizzie was a wonder at driving horses, and could handle any animal that was harnessed into her cart. Although she was firm in her commands, she had a natural empathy with horses and always seemed to get the best out of them. If the Townsleys always used good quality driving horses, then the vehicles to which they were harnessed matched them for quality. The gigs, carts and traps that the Townsleys owned were well made vehicles which ran easily on wheels that were fitted with iron or steel tyres to cope with the rough conditions of the roads of that time. Lizzie spent every working day driving one of these vehicles to outlying areas to sell such things as fish, pots, lino, or bedding to the villagers or farming folk.

There was a ready market waiting for her in these villages. None of the people that lived in the country had access to the ease of shopping that we take for granted today. They were dependent for basic food stuffs on what they could either grow on their own land, or buy from a nearby farmer. Small village shops stocked basic supplies such as tea, sugar, and other dried or household goods, but for a supply of fresh fish, or items of hardware, the country folk were dependent on the regular visits to their villages by the travelling folk that either came by horse and cart, or pedalled their goods from door to door on foot, like the old packmen and women.

"We all had to carry hawkers licences and these had to be produced whenever they were called for. We also had to take to a certain public place, our weighing scales and all other weighing instruments to be checked and stamped every year."

The travelling Townsleys were on the road every day, to face whatever conditions the weather brought, be it hail, rain, sleet or snow. In John's memory, those winters of many years ago, seemed to be far more severe than they are today. Most of the Townsley's carts were open to the weather, there were only covers to give protection to the goods that were being carried; the drivers had to rely on many layers of warm clothing, and their own resilient constitutions to get them through the worst of the weather. John recalled some of the winter conditions from the time when he was a young lad. *"The winters we used to get were very wet and very cold. There were always falls of snow and the becks used to freeze over for weeks on end. We used to jump off the carts and run alongside to get warm, especially when going up hill. You had to be well clothed with good footwear, and we were always well fed with a tea spoon of cod liver oil every morning. The country people used to say, I don't know how you and your sisters stand it. My sisters were all fit and healthy, most of them carried so little fat, they were all muscle with hard work, and doing a lot of walking every day. Yet they were always smiling and had a cheerful word for everybody."*

When John Townsley junior was a young lad of about seven, he used to go out into the "high country" with his favourite sister. *"I was a little boy when I used to go with my sisters, I liked to go with Lizzie best. She always had the best driving horse because she had the furthest to go. People used to ask if they had seen their relations in different parts of the country where we travelled. They would say, Will you be going to such and such a place this week, and they would ask us to deliver a parcel, and pass on the word that all was well with that particular branch of a family. We always got something to eat and drink off the country people, as they were very kind. They would give us tea and cake for only a few pennies for maybe two or three of us.*"

Sometimes the pangs of hunger struck at empty bellies before they could be assuaged at a friendly farm house, or maybe the coppers were not sufficiently available to spend on a cup of tea or a sandwich. *"We didn't touch the money that we took for the goods. That all had to be accounted for. I have seen us eating the fleshy part of a kipper to stave off the pangs of hunger until we got home. Sometimes after we had sold all the fish, we would pick up sacks of potatoes or turnips, maybe a bag of corn. We used to buy all our potatoes, and greens from country people and farmers. It was a case of you buy off us, and we'll buy off you. After the cart was loaded up, I would hold the horses head until my sister had lighted the candles in the lamps, and then climb aboard."*

Once the day's business was over, and the horse's head had been turned towards home, John's sister would say, *"Wrap that coat round you, and hang on tight. Hills, back lonnin's, moors and bridleways were all the same to her. She was in her element when driving these road hacks. She had the best of horses and strong harness, and her German muller whip. There was no woman born could drive and graft like her. At seven o clock at night in the depths of winter, it was black dark."*

On most days, there was a journey of between fifteen or twenty miles to reach home, when there was hardly another thing stirring on the rough roads. Sometimes, after they had been on the road since six o clock in the morning, it was nine at night before they drove the cart into the yard for the horse to be unharnessed, rubbed down and fed. To the travelling Townsleys, time meant nothing, they were expected to stay out until they had sold out of any perishables, or when hawking other SWAG, they carried on working until they had made a day's pay.

The lane and the yards were never left unattended. There was always at least two members of the Family that stayed at home to deal with anyone that came to buy, or just to have a look at a horse, a harness, or even some second hand clothes. *"Every member of the Family was equal to any situation, for there was always miscellaneous goods to sell from any of the buildings, Even if it was two women that were at home, they could do every type of dealing, even to selling horses."* There also needed to be someone at the yard in case anyone came with goods to sell, or sometimes to leave for a while against payment of a sum of money, for in the hard times of the twenties and thirties, the Family acted as pawnbrokers, and money lenders as well as in their more traditional dealing role.

Their work did not stop at the weekends, for as John recalled, *"the young women used to do all the washing, baking and cleaning at our houses at the weekends."* For this, the girls were rewarded with a shilling a week pocket money. When bed time came, it was upstairs to bed by the light of candles, for the luxury of a good night's sleep before they were up again at dawn to have their turnouts ready for another day on the road. But every year, the girls did have a special treat to look forward to; that was the annual trip that was organised by the Workington brass band committee, and was affectionately known as "The Town Band Trip."

"They used to look forward, once a year to the Isle of Man trip out of Workington. It was three shillings and sixpence steerage, that was up on deck in the weather, or five shillings in the saloon. The girls would wear their new burberry macs that cost fifteen shillings from the warehouse in Manchester. When they got back in the early hours of the morning, according to the tide, sometimes they could see our house as the ship lay off Workington waiting for high water to be able to get into the Prince of Wales Dock. When they got home, my mother would say to them, Get your good tug off, meaning their clothes. The breakfasts are on the table and there's five turnouts ready yoked and loaded waiting for the road. It's business and graft now, round your own districts."

If Ellen Townsley seemed hard on her family, it was only because she also had been brought up to accept that was a way of living that she regarded as normal. *"My mother was just short of six foot tall, and had been used to a hard life. She was frightened of nothing, animals or man. She thought nothing of walking at dark of night through frost and snow to meet the girls who were late getting home with their turnouts. She would walk through the woods and across footpaths, stopping to listen for the horses' feet. There were few cars on the roads in those days, and everywhere there was a ghostly silence. She would walk six or seven miles on freezing nights when they were hampered by snow-drifts and hard frost. She would carry a hammer, and studs in her pocket to hammer into the horses' shoes, if they were not studded up for the frost. This sometimes happened in the winter, if the weather suddenly changed."*

The lives of the daughters of the two neighbouring Townsley families were entirely different. While John Townsley's six sisters had to work hard at either travelling on their rounds, or by looking after the yard and working at home, his cousins who were Big Charlie's daughters had a much easier life style. *"My uncle, Big Charlie had several daughters who never hawked or worked, or even scrubbed the fish carts clean each night. Their father, mother and brothers idolised them. They had so many men folk who were the providers, and made the money so that the daughters just worked in the house cleaning and making the meals for the men. They were just like ladies, not like my sisters. Every one of them worked every day, and on into the night, but there was no jealousy with the girls, they all got on well together."*

Ellen Townsley was just as capable of sorting out money and family problems as her men folk had been. An old pig dealer who operated in the Cockermouth area recalled seeing Mother Ellen in fighting mood. *"There had been a family dispute, ten miles away in Cockermouth, and she went over to set the record straight. Now all the travellers living locally used to congregate in Jimmy Lowther's house. In walked Ellen Townsley through the front door, and the conversation in the crowded room stopped. Men took to the windows to get out, and some darted through the back door because they knew there was trouble in the air. She was in a fighting mood that night, and was*

Tales of a Lakeland Gypsy

there to sort things out. It was well known that she could handle herself, and kick up to touch the ceiling and budick off her hip. But it finally got sorted out, and she got paid the money that was owing to her in a deal."

Part of the problem had been caused by the unwritten law among travelling folk that they only sold fish and herring, which were classed as perishables, on their own territory. Sometimes there were contraventions when pit men, or "dyke back" men, tried to emulate the travellers ways. *"My people could all tell in a minute who were the true breeds, and who were not. Our cousins used to stray on our territory when selling herring or fish. If you were having a "gammy" day, you had to look for pastures new, but not your relations' patch. We had Harrington, Workington, lots of the villages in the high country, and the Families knew it. But when the others did stray, my mother would let them know to stay off."*

Through their business and graft in their own districts, the Townsley girls became well known to the farming and village communities. It was not only the goods for sale that they carried with them on their rounds, but they were also able to pass on news and messages from one family to another. This was much appreciated in the days when communication between isolated farms was difficult. News was part of the life blood by which their Family business flourished, for while out on their rounds, they always kept their ears open for news of anything that they might be able to turn to profit. They were always on the look out for old clothes, scrap metal or any furniture that was no longer needed. If the girls learned of any place that had any scrap metal to be collected, they made arrangements to buy it. Sometimes, they paid so much down and the balance was paid when the scrap was collected by one of the men folk.

The Townsleys also dealt with the road workers who trapped animals to supplement their meagre wages. In the rural areas of the Lake District, as in other parts of the country in the early years of the twentieth century, the road surfaces were rough and in need of constant repair. Gangs of road men were allocated stretches of road that they had to maintain. They were known as "lengthsmen." Grass verges backed by thick hedgerows divided farmland fields from the roads and each gang of road men regarded any game that was caught along their stretch as their rightful property. They made the most of this opportunity by setting snares and traps in the hedge bottoms to catch rabbits or pheasants. These were then sold to the Townsley travelling lasses that passed along their stretch of road.

Every day before the girls set off on their rounds, they were given a float of cash by Nellie, the eldest girl who managed the Family's finances. Farthings, halfpennies and a few silver threepenny, sixpenny or shilling pieces were carried in their bags. There were one or two sovereigns just in case there was something extra special that caught their eyes, so that they were able to pay for it in cash. At the end of the day when they returned from their travels, the cash bags were handed over, and the amount of float deducted to see what profit had been made that day. Every single penny was counted back into the pot on the table. While the counting was going on, the girls took the opportunity to pass on any information they had heard while they were out on their rounds. Village people used to gather about the Families carts and chatter about the

35

goings on in their areas while they were waiting to be served. The girls always had an ear cocked to hear if anyone in the district was selling up; if any new family had moved into the district, or if any had fallen on hard times and was likely to need some ready cash. The information was mentally stored, to be of benefit later. *"There was a NARK in every area in the country; the man who knew what was going on. He knew who had got a new driving turnout and if it was NAPPY or dodgy. The Families had these men giving them the news."*

The men folk gathered their information in much the same way. *"Even when having a little time off you had to be alert to anything that was going on. If the men folk went to the pictures in Workington, they would call first at various houses to see who had beneficial information. Life ran on news, who was looking for something and if the Family could supply it, we would."*

Every Friday night was CHUCKY night, for as John Townsley explained, part of the family income came from selling goods on CHUCK, [credit], and collecting in at the weekend when the Parish Relief money was paid. Money was only lent to those people who were trusted, and each driver of a turnout had their own CHUCKY book, because they knew which of their customers could pay back when the time came, or those that had property, land or assets to cover their debts. Some of their CHUCKY notes would read:

Laal Mary on the landing, crown's worth of fish, and a crown borrowed.

Mary up wide yard; no fish, borrowed ten HOGG.

Big MOTE through the JIGGERS; fish, three HOGG and borrowed ten HOGG.

"Everyone knew us in Low Harrington, and if they needed help, or something on CHUCKY, they could usually get it. We used to get the borrowed ROWDY [money] in with the CHUCKY fish money on a Friday night and Saturdays, and lend ROWDY and sell again on Monday."

One of the weekend jobs that had to be done involved skinning and selling rabbits that had been bought in during their travels. *"We would go into the village with two or three hundred rabbits. People clambered for rabbits and while three of us skinned, one took the ROWDY."* Rabbits could be skinned in a flash. The legs of the animals were broken, a nick made in the skin, which was then virtually turned inside out to finish with the skin being nipped off at the nose. *"A lot of folk cut the rabbits head off, but our Lizzie was so fast that she could peel the skin off in one piece."*

Another side line was the Family business of pawn broking where people pledged goods, or possessions against a sum of money until their Parish Relief was paid. *"We were known as all round business people, and we were into pawn broking, lending cash on goods taken in; horses, or anything else. We had a name second to none."* For the pawn broking, and money lending the Family charged an additional percentage for the service they provided. Friday night was the night that people came back to redeem their pawned goods, and that same evening business people who had borrowed money to open their shops on a Monday morning, came to repay their weekly loan, with interest.

Tales of a Lakeland Gypsy

Saturday was the Families reckoning up day. *"On a Saturday around five o clock when all the business had been done, Nellie would put the fish bills and the money received into a bag, and they would watch me go to our cousin's house next door. The door was always open, and they would shout, Come on in, its laal John come to pay the fish bill. The man in charge was my cousin with the same name as me. He was the banker for the paying and ordering of fish and herring from different ports around the country. He would reckon it all up, and then my cousin John would say, tell your mother and the lasses that it is all right. He would give me sixpence and maybe some sweets and a piece of fruit. There would be a dozen or so men all sitting round a large oval table with a big log fire burning; they were all talking about things in Romany while they were waiting for the women folk to make their tea."*

Saturday night was the night that the local Insurance men called at the houses down the lane. *"They were always wanting the Family to take out more insurance. The men folk would say, well boys, just get into the middle of the kitchen and give us a song and we'll see about doing business with you."* The family enjoyed music, and two of the insurance men that called were renowned for their singing. *"A little fella, Joe Tinnion was an ex miner and he was a good tenor that sang in the church choir; or his SIDEKICK would come. That was Stanley Douglas who was a good baritone CHANTER. They used to harmonise singing old fashioned songs like "Marta" and "The Pale Moon was Shining."*

After the singing, there was good food and drink, and the insurance men departed well fed, but maybe not always with any increase in their business. *"Both families used to like to hear CHANTERS, accordion players, melodeon players especially when they played the Scottish and Irish folk and country songs. Sometimes we used to get the tap dancers and the clog dancers. We had some good singers in the Clan. My cousin Charlie was always singing, and could play the fiddle. My sisters were in the church choirs and would sing at local concerts or pantomimes."*

Another Saturday night caller was the butcher, whose van was pulled by an ex-army horse with the initials WD stamped on its hoofs. Ellen Townsley would buy a fair lump of MASS [meat] from him, *"and then put the arm on him for a lump of potted meat for nix"*. Joe Yeowart was another butcher that called. John remembered the beautiful coach work and painted lines of the bull nosed Morris van that he used. *"We bought scrap meat off him. We bought from his slaughterhouse all his bones, skins and cow tailings."*

Mother Ellen ensured that Sunday was the day for the weekly dose of the working medicine. *"We had to take the working medicine every Sunday morning. It was a recipe that my mother made up using lemons and other fruit."* said John. Other Sunday morning activities included chopping up hay, carrots, turnips and mangolds for the horses. To this mixture of vegetables was added corn and PROVEN, honey and treacle, as well as a small measure of cod liver oil. There were also the candles to be made and the chalk blocks for giving the whitened edge to the doorsteps of houses, after they had been given their weekly scrubbing. *"We had proper moulds and mixing pots for these, and we sold the candles and chalk on our rounds."*

37

Tales of a Lakeland Gypsy

The Families were all members of the Church of England, but work did not stop on the Sabbath, although the Elders ensured that the children all made the long walk across the fields to attend the local Sunday School. *"We went twice on a Sunday and whatever we had, we took for the harvest festival. All the young people had to be confirmed, and some of the men folk cut the church yards to keep them tidy and to make hay to feed the horses. We also used to go to what was called Valence's Meeting House. This was on the west side of Harrington and I was about seven when we went there in the early twenties. The parlour was full of chairs and we sang hymns and after that, they would give us an apple and an orange. These were very kind, good people and were well thought of in the area. We had to walk back home across fields and through woods, but even on freezing starlit nights, we were not afraid to be out."*

The Family lived well. They kept some animals of their own such as hens, a few milking goats and a cow, and pigs that were butched by a local slaughterman when the time was ready. Add to that a plentiful supply of fresh fish, fruit and produce that was collected from the farms, and even in the poverty stricken times of the twenties, the Family never went short of food.

"We always used to have loads of hams and sides hanging up in the houses, and there was always others down in salt." John explained that the best hams for the Family were those that he described as FONKY or tainted, *"as the gentry might say. Those hams were high, but what a taste! The Families kept pigs and poultry, and sold hams to business people and shops. We always scranned well, that's eating. No one was ever turned away; that's how we got to know what was happening on the road. We had special mugs and plates for roadsters and tramps in one of the out buildings. Tramps were to be seen everywhere in those times. Even travelling people who were passing through the district used to call and get a good meal. There used to be scissor grinders, chanters, tin whistlers, even "tubs to mend" people. They were all men of the road with a tale to tell, what they had seen or heard in their travels. They all knew that they would be welcome to a good meal and a cup of hot strong tea. They would all come down the old Potters' Lonnin' knowing they were never, and I mean never turned away. Sometimes they would be kitted out with clothes and shoes that our Family had discarded when they got new clothes and footwear."*

Sometimes the girls would come back from travelling with army kitbags full of second hand clothes, which the Family called TUGGERY. It all had to be sorted before they could sell it again around the district. Dealing in second hand clothing was a lucrative part of Mother Ellen's family business. Many a time, the girls would go out with their traps loaded with the sorted TUGGERY, and as they sold one outfit, they would buy back the old one that it was replacing. They also dealt in new clothes and cotton print material which they ordered from the Lancashire mills which was delivered to the nearby Harrington railway station. Some of the second hand clothes that were bought in from the better off farming families, or the "gentry", were in excellent condition, and many of these would be kept for the families own use. *"In among the old TUG that they used to get in exchange for a couple of tea towels, or an apron, there were sometimes beautiful hats, or fur capes. The BARRY velour wide brimmed hats were in great demand. The ANTLE used to wear them pulled down over one YAK.*

Tales of a Lakeland Gypsy

Young FLATTY lasses used to come knocking on our door for these SCUFF MURRAYS, and Paisley scarves. But the SCUFF MURRAYS [hats] made of velour with wide brims were also much sort after by the BARRY ANTLE GENTRY. They would pay up to £10, and we were LIFTING them for a bit of drapery. Our lasses would steam them into shape with the steam from a kettle of boiling water." Men were as keen to get this type of hat as their women folk as it was considered fashionable to *"wear a dropped brim over one eye".* John takes quiet amusement at seeing the MOTES in the racing world wearing them at race meetings today.

Prized among the TUGGERY were cotton raincoats, for the Family had their own way of treating them to create an early form of the Barbour jacket that is now so popular with farmers, fishermen and other outdoor people.

"All the cotton raincoats were kept back for a special purpose. They used to brush on to all these coats, on a table, linseed oil, and then hang them up to dry in one of the buildings in the yard or up on the loft. As they dried, they would take them down and give them several more coats of linseed. We kept some for our own use, and then the rest were sold to farmers and other outdoor people. Once the coats had had this treatment, they were very light in weight, and could turn the water that would never get through. So it seems as though this was a Gypsy business that the "FLATTY's" cottoned on to."

At the right time of year, after the fell sheep had been brought down from their "heafs" to the the intake land of the farms to be sheared, Mother Ellen's daughters would visit many farms in the Ennerdale, Wasdale, and Eskdale valleys to buy the full clip. *"We would stay down in south Cumbria for a few days until we had bought as much wool as we could handle. We could buy wool for a penny a pound, and we could even buy a farmer's full clip at these prices."*

Mother Ellen made sure that her youngest son pulled his weight in the family business, and one of John's jobs when he was a young lad was to go with the flat cart to collect the hay and feed for the horses. A regular supply was obtained from the Furness brothers at the nearby Scaw Farm at Harrington. *"I used to go regularly for a load of hay, and carrots and bags of corn. It was a really old fashioned place, and the family were just the same. It was just like going home. Jimmy would say when I pulled in the yard, get what you want, I'll see your mother when I come up to the village. The hay was 2d or 3d a LEP. You gathered it all up in your arms and pressed it as much as you could; then you would roll some hay into a twine, and fasten it around. You had to get as much as possible; whether you did or not, it was all the same price. They gave us turnips for nowt."*

John attended the village school, but admitted that he was not the best of pupils for he was often to be found away on one of the carts, rather than sitting at his class room desk. *"Many's the time the School Board Man has been after me. He used to travel around on a bike."* It was a lengthy walk for the Townsley children to the school in the village. They had to make their way across fields and through woods, over stiles and swinging gates. The return was made at lunch time for the hot meal that Mother Ellen had waiting for them, and then it was back to school again for the afternoon session.

39

Tales of a Lakeland Gypsy

At night, Mother Ellen also made sure that John had his share of the jobs to do. There were horses to see to in the fields, stables to clean, out buildings to clear, and those horse drawn vehicles that were for sale had to be washed and polished to look their best. *"As soon as we were old enough, we had to do our share of the work. When I was a little lad in the early twenties, and also being the youngest, I sort of went with anybody in the horse turnouts, cars or small lorries when we got those. I went with them whether they were horse trading, OLD STUFFING [dealing in scrap and metals], selling fish and herring in the summer, hawking goods or selling coal. So I had a good grounding in the all round trade. There was never any time for hanging around with nothing to do. As one seasonal job faded, you knew what was coming up next."*

As the sisters grew up, married and each left home in turn, John assumed more and more responsibility for the family business. He recalled that when he drove home at the end of a long day, with a good animal between the shafts of his cart and a bag full of money, the miles meant nothing. *"The only thing you concentrated on was that driving hack in your cart; up hill, down dale, flying like the wind. There was no other traffic on the road, just nature all around, and a wave from the farmers in the fields. There was food waiting on the table and others to loose out the horse from the cart and see to its needs."* The horse would be walked up and down the lane, with heavy horse rugs over its back. Once it had cooled down, it was taken into the stable and rubbed down before being fed with the best PROVEN mixture and hay.

"I was coming home from the high country one day, when I met an old packman coming out of Lamplugh. They called him Billy Varey. He had a pack under his arm with hawking tackle in it. He used to walk fifteen or twenty miles a day, calling at farms on his way. I was just a boy then, and was coming back home loaded with scrap. I stopped, and he jumped on the cart and I dropped him near where the travellers were camping on the Cloffocks at Workington. Walking was done by a lot of people in those days, people taking orders to get things from shops, and walking out to deliver it."

In 1939, the war intervened, John was called up and Mother Ellen was left on her own. The sisters had all married, and She moved to Cockermouth to be near one of her daughters. *"The war time years broke up a lot of the two families. Many of them died, especially when I was away in the army and I never saw a lot of them again."*

Mother Ellen died in 1956 and John buried her at Harrington, close to other members of the Families. *"Travellers always like to be buried near to the road, and they have lots of verses on the stones. On the Townsley stone is carved the inscription, "THE LAST MILESTONE PASSED."*

Tales of a Lakeland Gypsy

Tales of a Lakeland Gypsy

Mother Ellen

41

Chapter Four

FISH FOR SALE

Selling fish was a long established tradition in both the Lowther and the Townsley families. Even today, a Townsley fish van can still be seen travelling to many districts in order to carry on the family business. The modern motor vehicle with its compliance to present day hygiene regulations, not only bears the family name, but also the date 1830. *"Yes that was the year we went into fish along with the other jobs such as horse trading."*

John Townsley recalled that unlike present times when there is a dearth of fish in the Solway, great shoals of herring used to come into these waters where they were caught and landed at the ports of Whitehaven, Workington, and Maryport.

A former resident of Maryport, who was born and brought up in a house on the harbour side, can remember that in the 1920's, the herring boats that came into Maryport harbour were so numerous, that she was able to cross from one side of the harbour to the other by walking on their decks. The fish were so plentiful that local people could freely help themselves to a basket of herring from those that spilled out as they were being unloaded from the boats. Small villages such as Allonby and Parton also had their own fishing fleets, and Allonby even had its own kippering house where the gutted herring were hung from racks to be smoked. over damped down fires. The old building still stands today, although it is now part of the premises given over to a riding school. Parton was another west Cumbrian village that developed a great reputation for herring fishing, and the catches that were brought ashore on to its sweeping beaches about seventy years ago, are still remembered as being some of the best herring that were ever landed along the Cumbrian coast.

Way back in those far off days of the mid nineteenth century, Chucky Bob Lowther's wife, Ellen, used to travel the 20 mile journey from her home at Whitehaven to the small fishing village of Allonby, to buy quantities of fish from the Solway fishermen. She drove her own horse and trap right on to the beach and alongside the boats, from where the silvery catch was loaded directly into her baskets in the trap. There is no harbour at Allonby, but situated as it is at the centre of a sweeping bay, the boats were dragged out of the shallowing waters and right up onto the shingled beaches by teams of powerful horses. It was by such a method that the boats could be brought almost alongside the kippering house and the fishermens' cottages.

The Townsleys bought their supplies of fish either from the local fishermen of Harrington, or from further afield from the busy fish quays on the north east coast of England or from Scotland. Improved communications and rail transport made this available to them. In the early part of the 20th century, the two Townsley families, that of Big Charlie and his brother John, could get fish delivered by rail from Aberdeen at

Tales of a Lakeland Gypsy

a price of £20 per ton. The quality of the fish was so high, that it maintained its freshness throughout its long journey. Fish that was unloaded at the fish quays in far off ports in the morning, arrived at Harrington by an afternoon train. A telegram to the Townsleys indicated when the fish had been despatched. The ice in which the fish was packed, dripped into melting puddles in the carts as it was collected from the station, to be driven to the Townsley store sheds.

When motorised transport became available to the Townsley brothers, John and Big Charlie, drove over the Border to Annan on some weekends to buy freshly caught plaice from the local Scottish fishermen. An indication of the quality of the fish was denoted by the red spots which *"were as large as a coin."* They loaded up the "dickies" [boots] of the cars with the fresh fish, the smell of which, mingled with that of sea weed. *"It was a refreshing smell to anyone that understands fish."* said John. But even those that understood fish, appreciated the sweeter scent of a natural air freshener that was used in the car. *"They hung bunches of honeysuckle in the front of the car, to get the sweet smell flowing through"*. This was deemed a more pleasant alternative to the nose wrinkling richness that permeated through from the "dickie" at the back of the car.

When the families of Big Charlie and John Townsley were old enough to take a responsible part in the running of the fish side of their business, it was Big Charlie's son John who looked after the ordering of the fish. He dealt with the wholesalers in Aberdeen and North Shields who bought the landed catches from the fleets of trawlers. *"He was the brainy one"* was the tribute paid to him by his cousin. *"He would send the money to the various fish docks for the fish or herring we had all had that week, and he would order fish or herring for the following week. It was the women who mainly carried out the fish selling"* said John Townsley.

Fish was taken all round each families' trading area, which in the case of John's family, included "the high country." *"We sold fish, and other wares all around the country. We used to call at the Anglers' Inn on the shore of Ennerdale Lake and buy a jug of tea and sandwiches, before going up the lake with the water lapping at the lakeside road. We called on all the hill farms, and up to Gillerthwaite at the foot of Pillar Rock. It was really wild country in winter, but we travelled every week."*

The Anglers' Inn had the proud boast that sportsmen who used to stay there, could actually cast a line into the lake from the windows of the Inn. Sadly, the Anglers' Inn no longer stands on the shores of "Sweet Ennerdale" as John remembers it. When plans were proposed to extract more water from the lake for industrial purposes, it was envisaged that the raising of the level of the lake would be necessary to satisfy an increasing demand for water. Like so many other Lake District reservoir projects, homes, inns and even churches were drowned to satisfy industrial demands. The Anglers' Inn was demolished, but needlessly as events turned out; for there were many objections to the plans. The proposal to raise the level of the lake was defeated after a public enquiry in 1980. Sadly, the Inn is now only a memory in the minds of older folk. Members of a younger generation that now venture their way along a rough lane to reach the lake shore, find that the site of the Inn is nothing more than a popular picnic

Tales of a Lakeland Gypsy

spot.

The journey to deliver fish to Ennerdale was relatively short when compared with the deliveries that were made by some of John Townsley's Elders who drove their carts from west Cumberland to Kendal market. Their journey from Harrington was long and difficult, for the horses and carts had to be driven over the steep and unmade surfaces of the Hardknott and Wrynose passes, and usually involved travelling overnight. It did however give them the opportunity to sell fish at some of the remote farms in the Eskdale valley, and thus establish trading contacts with the farmers for horses and other goods. *"Also travelling with them were other turnouts with horses tied up behind, or driven loose in front of them. These were for sale or exchange as they called at farms and hamlets. The journey from Harrington to Kendal was about 58 miles through the southern Lake District. When they returned from Kendal, to Whitehaven and Harrington, they traded horses, and SWAG on the way back."*

The Townsley fish business was very much a seasonal trade; they were dependent upon the supplies that were available to them. Herring was one of the staple fishes sold in the business. During a good herring season which resulted in a glut of the silvery fish, the surplus were cured in one of the buildings along the lane. There they stayed, packed in their barrels of salt, to be taken out and sold during the autumn months, or used as extra food for the Families during the winter. The herring season used to start in May, and it carried through until late August. In those pre-fridge and freezer days, catches of newly caught fish were eagerly awaited. *"At first, the country people were desperate for herring, but they used to drop out after a few weeks. But we kept at it until late August or early September."*

News that the herring were on their way from some far distant fish dock was delivered to the Townsley's in a coded message. It was brought by a navy uniformed telegraph boy who pedalled furiously up the Harrington hill to the Townsleys' lane. His pill box hat was worn jauntily aslant, as the energy expended to propel the cumbersome and heavy bicycle brought colour to his cheeks.

The arrival of the telegram brought immediate action on the part of the Family to get organised to meet the afternoon train. *"The herring came into Harrington on the afternoon train arriving at about four o clock. You had to be there, on time, at our local railway station when the train came in. The herring were packed in KITS, [barrels]. They were covered over the top by sacking. Different people would try and slip a few herring for themselves out of the top of the barrels."* Some of the barrels were designated for John's family, while the others were for Big Charlie.

"People used to queue up at the railway station yard where we used to start and sell them. We once had the shafts of a flat cart broken in the crush, with people swinging and crushing to get served."

As well as the carts that were used for selling herring at the station, there were always two turnouts waiting to bring fish to the Townsley fish store, where other members of the family were waiting. Those turnouts, with horses already harnessed in the shafts, became the centre of a frenzy of activity as each was loaded up with five or six barrels of fish; the drivers keen to get away with their deliveries in the afternoon

44

Tales of a Lakeland Gypsy

and early evening. *"You could have a hundredweight of fish on a cart, for about one pound, and you could also have a load of SWIMMERS, [herring] for one pound fifty pence. [THIRTY HOGG] to two pound [TWO RIDGE]. You grafted away, and when you got your cost price, or the ROWDY you had paid out, it was all profit after that."*

Once the initial selling rush at the station was over, and the other turnouts were speeding on their way to the distant villages and farms, the remaining women members of the family stayed at the station, where they were helped by a railway porter to load the remaining fish on to the carts. These were taken back to the lane, where the fish were put into store to keep cool, ready for the next day's early morning delivery.

The fish were sorted out, usually by size, and packed into different boxes. *"Some people wanted Parton herring and some Loch Fyne and some East coast herring."* This was in spite of the fact that all the divided herring were from the same delivery. *"You could be splitting herring, and folk would say, I'll have some of those large Scottish herring. You got less of course for your money, but all the herring had come from the same place. But you couldn't tell them that. It was the same with fish. Some eccentric people would point to a box of fish and say, I will have so much of that fish, giving it a name of a more scarce and expensive type. You could not contradict them, and you could not tell them otherwise.*

The fish delivered one day were just as fresh and good when we set off with them next morning. We left at six o clock in the morning, and delivered right through the hot summers' days. We went through farms, villages, bye roads; flying with these horses till come early evening when maybe we only had one box left. The herring were still in lovely condition, but they all had to be sold as a new consignment would have been delivered to the railway station that day."

At the end of the day, the members of the family who were out on their rounds knew where they could unload any quantities of fish that were still left unsold. *"There was always one or two people in every district would take large amounts of fish for themselves or their relatives. They would say, let us have it a bit cheaper for the amount we are buying off you. And we did."*

In the thirties, the normal price for the fish that the Townsleys sold seems remarkably cheap compared with today's inflated prices. Their price list read,

Kippers.. a penny or twopence a pair

Bloaters and red herring.. penny each

cod, plaice, and haddock on the bone,

filleted white and brown fish.. eightpence a pound.

"That's in old money of course" John explained.

The Family made an attempt to cut out the middle man in their herring business by catching the fish for themselves. *"We once bought a small boat to catch our own herring locally. We got a load of them, but people were getting tired of looking at herring by then. Another time we bought a boat load of herring at the end of the season.*

45

Tales of a Lakeland Gypsy

We made kippers and bloaters with some, and swamped the countryside with the rest selling them at forty or fifty for a shilling."

John recalled the reputation that his Uncle Charlie had for selling fish, *"My uncle, Big Charlie used to shout as he sold fish or herring in Brigham. And they could hear him across the river Derwent in Great Broughton, a distance of over a mile away."* Customers were otherwise summoned to the fish carts by the ringing of a hand bell. *"I still have some good fish bells that we used to ring. They saved us time, and also your legs, when calling on customers in towns and villages."*

In John's opinion, *"Fish in the old days, and up to the last war was far better than it is today. The slime and the sweet smell was something else, yes a real healthy fish smell".* He explained that with SWIMMERS *"You could batter through villages and farm houses all day, and they were in real good condition at the end of the day. Today I just look at them, and turn away. I have seen boxes of kippers, when at their best in June, saturated in natural fat, the fish carts were swimming with it. They are not like that now. You could put some kippers out of the cart in the sun, and they would cook. Then you could SCRAN them."*

As fish stocks have declined in the Solway over the last twenty or thirty years, many reasons have been put forward to explain the loss. Pollution of the sea off the Cumbrian coast by chemicals, heavy metals, untreated sewage, oil, as well as radioactive material has gone on for years. The discharges have not only come from outlets within Cumbria, but from further south, where effluent from industrial Lancashire discharges into the Irish Sea. The force of winds and tidal drift sends more pollutants to add to Cumbria's own. Once in the shallowing Solway, it tends to stay; for the narrow outlet of St George's Channel to the north is insufficient to allow a good through flushing tidal action.

Pollutants can sink to the sea bed where they are contained within the sand, only to be stirred once more into action by frequent gales and storms. In John's opinion, the herring left the Solway in numbers because of the slag that was tipped into the sea from the steel works at Moss Bay near to Workington. Gas was also discharged into the water from the same plant. *"As herring like clean water, they left the Solway, and have never returned in the large shoals."*

Easter was the busiest time of year for the Townsley's fish sales, with Easter Friday being the traditional fish eating day. *"The religious period of Easter was a very hectic time for fish. All denominations used to eat lots of fish over this religious season. We used to take on extra help because we had turnouts going all over the countryside. It was a busy time. The main day was Thursday before Good Friday, so a lot of road miles and territory had to be covered in a very short time. The orders were wrapped in greaseproof paper, and put in the boxes in rotation for delivery on each of the rounds. There was also the fish that had not been ordered. Plaice and flat fish was filleted at home by others before leaving the yard. Many days, the girls came back in around midnight with their horse turnouts. The lamps were lit up on both sides of the carts, as they travelled through the quiet countryside in the black of the night. Nothing would be moving, nothing stirring in the blackness of the night, but when the horses heads were*

46

Tales of a Lakeland Gypsy

turned for home, then it was a case of holding tight as the horses did their stuff."

During the Easter period, the Townsleys had as many as seven or eight fish carts on the roads, as well as some of the lasses hawking the fish round the narrow alleys, and rows of terraced houses; selling the fish from baskets often carried on their heads. The girls used to hawk kippers as well as herring from their baskets. *"My sisters would empty boxes of kippers into baskets at the railway station, and carry the baskets on their heads. They would do the streets of Low Harrington in this way. There used to be landings, nooks, squares, and small entries to the houses. With a basket you could get right up to the doors."* One of John's sisters whom he described as *"a lean blood stick"*, was adept at selling fish from a basket carried on her head. *"It was all action when she got started. She would carry baskets of dried fish on her head when selling in the towns, then darting back to another sister with a cart in the streets to refill her basket. Fine days, wet days, frost or snow, they just went out to make money."*

If there was no fish to be obtained when the boats were port bound as a result of bad weather, that was no occasion for the Townsleys to take a day off work. There was still money to be made as they drove out in their turnouts to sell their pots and pans, rolls of lino [PONGO], and other staple goods from their hawking packs. They were still able to sell some fish at such times, for then they were able to resort to the smoked or salted fish that had put down for just such emergencies, when there was an interruption in the delivery of their normal supplies.

Many local West Cumbrian fishermen used to take their own small catches that were made on each fresh tide, "down the lane," to sell to the Townsleys. The locally bought fish included the Solway skate, plaice, haddock, and hake. When these were brought in on a Sunday night, there were hours of hard, finger tearing work to be done to skin the skate to prepare it for sale the next morning. When John was a youngster he had to learn how to fillet any kind of fish. *"I could skin the thorn backs and waste off the skate when I was eight years old and take orders and deliver down in the town."*

On other occasions, fish was the currency that was used to pay local people who brought in grass cuttings or hay for fodder for the Townsley horses. *"Men used to cut grass in parks and other open spaces to make hay for us, and we would give them fish or herring in return."*

When the second world war broke out in 1939, John was called up to join the army. Two of his sisters attempted to carry on the business, but with the restrictions that were imposed by the lack of man power and fuel, as well as increased potential danger from war time activities, the fish became difficult to obtain. Eventually, both of his sisters married, and there was no one left of John's immediate family able to carry on with the business. He sold out his share of the business to his cousins, who are, along with another branch of the Townsley family, still in the fish trade today.

47

Fish for sale!

Chapter Five

HARD TIMES AT HARRINGTON

John Townsley was born at Harrington, which was once a busy port on the Cumbrian coast, but is now a sprawling village on the outskirts of its larger neighbour, Workington. *"It was a small place where I was born and bred and went to school. There were six churches, and quite a number of other denominations such as the Band of Hope, the Salvation Army, the Plymouth Brethren, and they were all well attended. The Salvation Army Singers used to come down our lonnin' to sing and pray; especially at Christmas. They were always well done by as the Elders thought highly of these good people."*

Inevitably, with the passing of the years, Harrington has undergone a considerable change in its character, losing its identity over and over again, as agriculture was replaced by industry, which in its own turn, declined. The rows of terraced houses that were built in close proximity to the harbour basin once accommodated a population of almost 4,000 at the onset of the 20th century; but most of these houses have now been demolished. Their former sites have been cleared to make way for the development of an extensive area of recreational land located to the south of the once busy port. To replace rows of terraced houses, suburban type estates now extend over the rising ground to the north and south, while Harrington's former industrial sites have completely vanished.

Harrington and its lords of the manor is recorded from shortly after the Domesday Book. The ownership of the land changed a number of times, until the powerful Curwen family, whose home was at Workington Hall, became lords of the Manor of Harrington from the sixteenth century. Along with the title was possession of the harbour and the mining rights of all minerals in the Manor. Of these, coal and iron were the most important. As early as 1749, which was five years after Bonnie Prince Charlie tried to regain the English throne, coal was being mined in and around Harrington. It was led away from the pits to the harbour on the backs of pack horses, and there it was loaded into many of the boats that were registered at the port, to be shipped to Ireland.

It was John Christian Curwen who developed the coal trade to such an extent, that the harbour was brought into prominence as one of the most important on the Cumbrian coast. By 1800, over 60 ships were registered at the port of Harrington. The harbour was a bustling area of life and activity; of dirt and danger, where the hours of work were hard and long. Ropes littered the quay sides, the water of the harbour basin was covered with the black scum of coal dust; the reek of rotting fish mingled with that of steamy perspiring bodies as tubs and carts of coal were discharged into the waiting holds.

Tales of a Lakeland Gypsy

In 1840, the harbour duties imposed on vessels were *"chargeable according to the registered tonnage thereof. To any part whatever with Coals*

For Harbour tonnage, ninepence per waggon

For Harbour Light, three farthings per Waggon."

In addition to the busy harbour, there were also two ship building yards, a ropery, and a copperas works which employed over 100 people to make the chemical, ferrous sulphate, which was also known as green vitriol. The copperas works gave its name to the area of Harrington which is still known as Copperas Hill, where there were two long rows of terraced houses.

"These were rather peculiar houses because the bedroom quarters in some of the houses were let into the walls." John Townsley was able to recall.

Copperas Hill was a favourite camping area for travelling Gypsy families. *"They used to do business with us. My people used to say they could live off practically nothing. The old rabbit skins that they used to collect would have the rabbit's head still on it. They would cut the head out, no matter how old, and make soup with them with herbs out of the field. My dad was offered some soup one day, but he refused, and when he saw how they made it, he left their caravan and threw up."*

Harrington was a close knit community in the late 1800's, having at that time 16 inns or hotels that were licensed to sell drink. There were two breweries in Harrington to keep the inns well supplied with ale and by 1900, the number of drinking establishments had increased to 20. Many of the pubs were clustered around the harbour side which ensured that they were well patronised by the visiting seamen as well as the local people. *"It was a real rough place at nights and at weekends, that's where the seamen, the fishermen, dockers and miners used to drink. Some of the public houses were right on the harbour side, and men were in and out of them all day long. They fought all the time down there in Low Harrington."*

The influence of the harbour area is reflected in many of the names of the pubs that were so well patronised. Among them were the Ship Hotel, the Ship Inn, the Ship Launch on Stanley Street, and the Ship Launch at Sibson's place, while on Quay Street there was the Harbour Hotel.

It was this growing area of prosperity on the west Cumbrian coast that attracted members of the Lowther and Townsley Gypsy families, and persuaded them to give up their travelling and settle there. It provided them with a niche for their dealing activities in scrap, clothes, pots and pans, and other essential household wares. Providentially, they were aided in the expansion of their dealing trade by the opening of the Whitehaven Junction Railway in 1847. This made it easy for them to receive goods that they ordered from the mills and factories of Lancashire and Staffordshire, and also enabled them to despatch scrap, old clothes and skins to destinations all over the country.

Harrington was very much a village of two parts, for while High Harrington, where the Townsleys lived retained much of its agricultural environment, Low Harrington was the industrial area and included the harbour and the iron works.

50

Tales of a Lakeland Gypsy

"There used to be landings, nooks, squares and small entries. Low Harrington was a little town on its own with the harbour and the coal boats. There were butchers, pubs, barbers, and shops of all kinds. Our men used to buy scrap metals off the boats. We had something going in Low Harrington every day. Everybody knew us, and if they asked us for something on CHUCKY, they would get it. We got loads of scrap out of that little community."

The two minerals that were of any importance in the Harrington area were ironstone and coal. The former was mined a little distance away in the ore deposits on the fringe of the Lake District and transported to the four furnaces of the Harrington Iron Works, where it was converted into iron.

Only a short distance to the south of Harrington, some bands of coal of the quite extensive West Cumberland coalfield outcropped along the coast. This afforded the opportunity for local people to engage in coal digging for their own benefit, or to collect the sea coal which was washed ashore by the tide. This is a practise that is still continued into present times. *"We used to let turnouts to the people who were gathering the sea coal. It used to wash up on the beach in great heaps."* Nowadays, as one looks over the green expanse of reclaimed land, it is difficult to imagine the rows of terraced houses, and the industrial site that once provided homes and employment for about 250 men in 1900.

Coal mining, as opposed to coal digging was a dangerous occupation, for while there were some drifts of coal that could be reached from the surface, most of the commercial coal was obtained from deep sunken pits from which a number of workings extended under the sea. The roof supports for the narrow tunnels through which the miners crawled, were made out of sturdy pillars of coal. Some of the mine managers, greedy to maximise the amount of coal that was dug out of the mines, ignored the safety factor of the adequate roof supports of the tunnels and ordered the miners to dig into these pillars to extract more coal. The consequences of this disregard for the mens' safety, inevitably caused the tunnels to collapse, the weakened structures gave way, for an intial seepage of sea water to become a flood which drowned both workings and men. This was a major cause of loss of life of the workers, as well as those that occurred due to asphyxiation, or explosions caused through the accumulation of gas and firedamp.

In 1838, the Cumberland Paquet reported an explosion at John Pit where 40 men and boys lost their lives. *"all the sufferers, save only three were burned to death. Harrison Kaye was literally blown to pieces. All his clothes were rent from his body save the socks on his feet."*

John Townsley recalled some of the descriptions of Harrington of the 1800's and early 1900's that were passed down to him through the stories of his Elders.

"In the 1800's grass grew over many of the streets of Harrington, and many of the windows of the houses had no glass in the windows. Some were boarded up, while others had old bags nailed across them. In the hard times, no one had anything at all. All the working class were the same with poverty and hunger. We supplied the colliers and the seamens' families with old clothes because they could not afford anything

else."

Some of the Harrington folk used to try and implement their low wages by carrying out part time work, by seeking employment with some of the farmers in the surrounding country areas, in busy seasonal times of the year. This did not bring them any great monetary reward, for farm workers were no better off financially than those who worked in industry. *"Some poor people used to work for farmers in the fields. They were paid 1d or 2d in old money for weeding and thinning stitches of turnips from one hedge to another. They were on their hands and knees for hundreds of yards. It was slavery."*

By the turn of the 20th century, only three of the previous fifteen or so operational pits in the Harrington area were still working, yet they still provided employment for about 450 men. As some of the pits closed and the miners lost their jobs in areas near to their homes, they had to turn elsewhere to seek work in the remaining pits of the Cumberland coalfield. This was no easy matter, for the lack of public transport made commuting virtually impossible. Some of the men moved inland to seek work in the slate quarries of the Lake District where they actually lived in slate huts at their workplace, and only returned home at the end of their week's work on Saturday afternoon.

With such a dependence by the workforce on a single industry, the pit strikes that took place between 1921 - 26, meant that poverty was rife among the Harrington community, making life harder in those already hard times. The causes of the miners' strikes were based in the appalling conditions in which they were expected to work, and the reduced wages that were imposed on the men by mine owners, who were themselves experiencing financial difficulty in an already declining industry.

The mines' work force of that time had become quite elderly as a result of the huge losses of men on the battlefields of Europe during the first world war. Denied and deprived of the injection of energetic younger men, the older and less physically fit were unable to meet the economic productivity levels demanded by the owners that might have kept the mines financially viable. Another setback occurred across the Irish Sea, for Ireland which had been for many years the traditional importer of coal from Cumberland, imposed an import duty on British coal thus making it more expensive. Other factors contributed to the difficulties of the coal industry, such as a fall in the local population numbers which reduced the need for coal as a fuel, and foreign competition from cheaper imported coal. The combination of these circumstances made the home supplied product less financially attractive.

Many colliery owners still wanted to maintain their own incomes, and responded to this decline in their market by reducing wages and lengthening the working day of the men they employed. The miners retaliated in the only way possible; they withdrew their labour. *"In the 1921 and the 1926 coal strikes when the miners stopped working, we had a load of miners working for us. We got permission from the landowners. They were mostly working in the Copperas Hill area above the coast between Harrington and Lowca."* Charlie Townsley, who returned from Canada to help out with the family business when his dad's health was failing, was the one to get the striking miners to

Tales of a Lakeland Gypsy

work for the Family. *"He was the brains behind organising the miners who were on strike, to work for us. He got them to dig coal out of the small drifts on waste land, some of them were on our land. He had the monopoly of any coal that was dug out."*

Charlie Townsley hired the miners, paid their wages for working for the Family, negotiated the price of the coal per ton and exercised his rights over the dispersal of the coal. He also bought coal in from miners who were operating their own small coal drifts. *"I used to go with them in the 1926 coal strike as a little boy, and come back black, covered with coal dust. That was a bad year for the Family because we lost both my dad and Charlie within six months."*

The Townsleys not only had horses and carts to lead the coal away, but by that time had also acquired small Ford lorries, and during these years of strife, they supplied coal to almost everybody in the area, for it was virtually impossible to get the fuel in any other way. *"We supplied farmers in outlandish areas, and we also had the contract for supplying the Workington brewery."*

Mother Ellen looked after the YOKES [carts] and small lorries that came from the diggings heavily loaded down with coal. They were weighed on the little weigh bridge at the Harrington railway station. Even then, the Family principle of looking after themselves was to the fore.

"She also SQUARED the station master to TOUCH for extra weight."

John Townsley remembers hearing his Elders say that this period of depression was like a little gold rush for the Family. *"The people were desperate for BLACKIES [coal], and we couldn't keep up with it, so we had to recruit more YAGGERS to dig the coal out. We had even started to load railway trucks to send the coal to other places. We made a lot of money because we controlled and ran the miners digging the coal out for us to sell."*

The twenties and the thirties were indeed times of great hardship for the people of Harrington as the effects of the Depression hit home. *"Those who survived this era of appalling suffering and despair still remember, with an almost corrosive bitterness, the poverty they were compelled to endure, often for years at a time, and the blank monotony of prolonged unemployment. In the grey streets of the mining villages, grey faced ex - miners and their families went hungry and aged prematurely; if their bellies were empty, the pawn brokers shops were full. Enormous physical and psychological damage was done to the unemployed. Poverty, malnutrition and bad housing conditions lowered resistance to disease. Many miners lived in old and damp terraced cottages, often back to back, without baths, an indoor water supply or indoor sanitation. in these slum conditions, disease flourished and in Cumberland the rates for tuberculosis and infant mortality were well above the national average."* [West Cumberland Coal - Oliver Wood].

Even during Harrington's earlier period of prosperity when the iron works, the pits and the harbour trade were all in full swing, the low wages that were paid to the workers afforded little opportunity for people to save any money to act as a buffer against even harder times of the Depression. In order to survive those years, some of

53

Tales of a Lakeland Gypsy

the Harrington people took to scavenging the beaches for sea coal or driftwood for heating. They collected anything edible that was freely given by the tides, or scoured the beaches for anything that was usable. With long hours of time on their hands, there was little else to do. They walked the country lanes and gathered the fruit from the hedgerows, or mushrooms from the fields. *"They gathered everything they could get for nowt, that they could put into glass or pot jars and save for the winter. They used to gather driftwood that was washed up after the gales, and they were down on the shore carting up anything that was useful. Down at the harbour, people were always waiting for our families, week after week, year after year. It was pure poverty due to unemployment. The queues at the Dole offices in West Cumberland stretched for yards and yards along the streets. They queued for the Parish Relief or free meals or handouts. It was terrible. The people were literally starving, and these were the people we got our living off. They knew they could get herring or rabbits from us. To the ones that we really knew for years, and could trust, they could get a HOGG, that's a shilling, or HALF A SLAT, that's half a crown on loan, and fish on CHUCKY until the weekend. It was all CHUCKY to the weekends when they got their mean test money, or Parish Relief, call it what you will. We got our living from the money they got from the dole or the Parish Relief. It was already spoken for; they already owed it. They had to pay up or they got no more. Some would say if they missed a week, "Honour bright Miss Townsley, I will pay you next week." They were grim days. We used to loan money with very little profit. How could you do anything else when life was such a struggle? My sisters used to help them out all they could up on the landings of Rose Hill, up the Arches, all the different parts of that quaint old fashioned sea town called Harrington."*

The poverty and the inadequate housing inevitably gave rise to sickness and disease. Many of the diseases that are unheard of today through advances that have been made in the fields of improved housing and medicine, were common and took a great toll on family resources.

"Poor people's children seemed to get all sorts of diseases, like ringworm. And every week, they used to buy paraffin oil, to wet the childrens' hair for head lice. They would take them outside and comb the hair through with a fine tooth comb."

In 1901, one of John's sisters was taken ill with a severe attack of diphtheria, which was common enough in those days, but is barely heard of now. *"She was only very young, and they took her to the old Ellerbeck Hospital on the outskirts of the town, and my mother had to stay with her."* Ellerbeck was an isolation hospital, which was known locally as the Fever Hospital. There was no ambulance service to carry the sick to and from hospital, *"They drove her to the hospital, well wrapped up and on my mother's knee, in a horse and trap. They had to go down farm lanes, over the footpath of Poorhouse Moor, and across fields to get to the hospital. When she finally recovered, the horse turnout picked my mother and sister up to bring them back home."* From his own memory, John Townsley recalled the difficult days of the twenties and thirties. *"The poverty and sickness, you could smell it. TB was rampant. They had no firing for heat, there was desolation everywhere. The old terraced houses were in bad repair. They were damp and the wet got in through the weatherbeaten windows and doors. People were dying of hunger and suffering from malnutrition. People used to walk*

Tales of a Lakeland Gypsy

miles with their kids to houses in the country for free soup and a bit of bread."

John Townsley recalled that there was a wealthy family called Chance who lived at Winscales House, whose daughter made soup for the poor people everyday. *"Others used to walk up to our houses when they had not a bite of food in their own house. There was despair and gloom everywhere. This was how it was, year in and year out, just endless poverty, and these people and their children were really poorly clothed. We could have a load of fish, pottery and new clothes but no one with the money to buy it."*

Yet many of these people overcame the difficult times, and in a somewhat philosophical frame of mind, John Townsley queries how a modern generation would fare if presented with those problems in their every day lives.

There was one Harrington farmer by the name of Joe Wilson from Whins Farm, who used to do a lot of business with the family. They found he was a strict man, but kind, and in the hard times when many people were forced to take to the roads, Joe would allow roadsters and tramps to sleep in one of his barns, or one of the cow byres, where, if the heat from the animals made it really warm, the smell was assaulted the nasal senses. The roadsters were always checked for tobacco and matches before they were allowed to enter the barns, and if any were carried, they were confiscated and only returned when the roadsters were ready to move on. John recalled a tale that Joe told about two roadsters that stayed in one of his outbuildings at the time of the second world war. *"The one was a man, the other was a woman. The next morning when Joe opened the byre door, the couple walked out carrying a bundle. She had a new born baby wrapped up in some hay. They took to the road, and away they went. In Scotland, roadsters like these used to be called Highland Trippers. We never gave a thought about what people must have thought about us with our tackle. We had the best of everything when there was so little around."*

Yet times did improve and the Townsley turnouts continued to do business in the harbour area even after the ships had gone, the mines closed down and the iron furnaces had breathed their last. *"We had a business turnout every day selling fish, most of it on CHUCKY to be paid at the weekend. We had two turnouts down on a Friday night, one was selling hares and rabbits which we skinned. We could sell two hundred couple of rabbits, as well as pheasants and hares to the gentry. The other cart sold second hand clothes of all kinds which were in regular demand. People also came to pay their CHUCKY and borrowing money, and place their orders for the next week."*

In more recent times, John Townsley spoke to a Harrington resident about the hard times. *"I met an old man in Harrington down by the harbour, and he said I have heard my parents say that the biggest part of this small community down here on the waterside would not have survived if it had not been for the Townsley families helping them out when they were facing starvation and hunger."* John added that the family motto had always been to never turn anyone away, always help the poor and the needy, *"and this they did during the times of hardship in Harrington."*

Chapter Six

NEAR THE KNUCKLE

To many none Gypsies, or FLATTIES as John Townsley calls them, there is an air of mystique and suspicion that surrounds the lives of those who follow a travelling life-style. Many travellers show a disregard for accepted rules of a shackled society. Some members of this society who conform to its demands, regard the attitudes of travellers as an affront to all they stand for. Others however, may grudgingly admit to feelings of envy for a life style they could themselves embrace.

The "here today, gone tomorrow", way of life that many travellers adopt makes it difficult for a slow moving legal system to catch up with those who operate on the wrong side of the law. The fact that for generations many Gypsy families have sailed very close to the legal wind, has created feelings of curiosity, bewilderment, exaspera-tion and even anger among those watching from the sidelines. To these may be added the elements of fear and intolerance that are brought about from a lack of understand-ing of a different culture, while the residue of childhood threats. "The Gypsies will take you away if you're naughty", can rouse feelings of suspicion and apprehension. The Lowthers and the Townsleys were no different from any of the other Gypsy families whose activities, especially in the sporting world, were "near the knuckle" as the old saying goes.

The Gypsy gatherings that were held throughout the Lakes counties in years gone by, afforded the opportunity for the young men to test each other out; while on a much smaller scale, such gatherings were regular events down the lonnin' where John Townsley lived. He recalled that every weekend down the Potters' lonnin', many of the local characters, some of whom were real "hard cases", gathered to have a crack. High in priority was the chance to discuss any deals that were going on, and the opportunity to cast an eye over the lurcher dogs and the horses that the Families had for sale. There was also a display of proud, strutting, fighting cocks to tempt many of the local "cockers" to part with their money.

Cock fighting was made illegal in Britain in 1835, but even after that date fighting birds were kept in many secret locations throughout the county, as well as down the Townsley lane. When a few gambling men were among the gathered crowd, there was always the possibility of a fight being arranged with a subsequent bet on the Mains. During the years before the sport becameg illegal, cock fighting enjoyed the patronage of members of both the gentry and the clergy in the Lake Counties. Even after "cocking" was made illegal, there was a reluctance on the part of many country folk to give up the so called sport. Until the latter years of the 19th century, many country school boys were still expected to take their "cock penny" to school on Shrove Tuesday, as a welcome supplement to the school master's wage.

Tales of a Lakeland Gypsy

Sir James Lowther was one of the Cumbrian nobility who was responsible, along with others, for building and maintaining the cock pit at Carlisle which was in regular use. It was customary for cock fights to be held as a curtain raiser to the horse race meetings that took place at the Swifts race course in Carlisle. This gave the opportunity for the gamblers to make a few pounds in side bets on the cock fights before the racing began.

Two acts of parliament outlawed the "sport", along with bull baiting, and badger baiting in 1835, and 1849. It was believed that bull baiting, by which a tethered animal was attacked from all quarters by a pack of fighting dogs, rendered the meat more tender for human consumption. Although this activity ceased almost immediately with the new law, cock fighting proved harder to stamp out, while badger baiting still goes on to this day. There are murmurs that in remote areas of Cumbria, secretly arranged cock fights continue as well.

In 1888. the Worshipful Chancellor Ferguson, presented a paper on Cockfighting to the Cumberland and Westmorland Archeological and Antiquarian Society.[Transactions Vol 1X Art XX1X]. The paper contained a letter, which was written in 1887, from an anonymous writer, to an anonymous recipient. It indicated that the sport was alive and thriving, long after the acts of abolition.

April 1887

Dear _____

I am in receipt of yours, not being a cock fighter, only being led into by knowing Dick _____ so well and finding him money and being fond of sport, on two occasions I made a Main for him for £100 a side, shew 21 Cocks in, for also £5 per battle, the weight 4lb 4ozs up to 5lb 4 ozs two days fighting: out of the 21 cocks 17 caught, we fought nine battles one day and eight the other. The first Main was drawn, the second we won by three, the Cocks were weighed on the pit ready for work, they fought in Silver.

Now these Cocks were taken from their walk, say today, Friday, and fought about Monday or Tuesday week - say the cock was 5lbs weight or a little under at the time he was taken up, he would fight 4lb 4 ozs or so. On the first part of their training was cut a little off their wings and tail, then Senna tea to drink until say Tuesday, cut their spurs short and spar them with small boxing gloves tied on their heels - On Tuesday they get their medicine, the very best Turkey rhubarb and magnesia about the thickness of your first finger, in fact more than would quickly operate on you or me, next day, Senna tea again and sparring. They get very much reduced by Friday, all the fat out of them - after that they give them new milk and bread made of eggs and loaf sugar &c, in fact, everything that is good, the very best malt barley and so on - you would be astonished how they thrive each day.

They fought single battles for £5 or £10 and what they call four Mains that is 4 Cocks, of course the winner had to get two battles."

Silver spurs were used for the fights, not so much for their prestigious value, but because cuts healed better from wounds inflicted by silver spurs. It was important that they were correctly fitted, for in the fight, the dominant bird attempts to seize its opponent by the hackle, and while holding him down, use his spurs to attack the head of his foe. To do this, he has to kick or spur, and risk inflicting injury to himself if the spurs are incorrectly fitted. *"A game cock in training will be all right and well in three to four days after receiving several wounds."* By comparison, the bird's own natural spurs cause bruising in addition to the cuts, and are much slower to heal. Another of the properties of silver spurs is that on *"entering the brain, they kill at once"*, while *"natural spurs cause bruising and a lingering death."*

In the early years of the 20th century, cock fighting still went on the the Cumbrian town of Cockermouth where there was a cock pit in an old building at Butts Fold, in St Helens Street. The building is no longer there, but old memories can recall what went on.

"Inside this building they made all sorts of swills and baskets out of saplings. Inside there was a boiler to steam the saplings to make them more pliable. The windows of the building were blacked with dolly blue so that people couldn't look inside. To make sure that children didn't go in, they were told that witches and ghosts lived inside. The pit was dug out of the earth floor and covered over with board and the waste that came off the saplings. The spurs were all kept in the case of the grandfather clock at the home of the man who owned the building." John was given this information by a member of the family.

Although Townsleys bought and sold fighting cocks as one of their many business activities, John claims that none of his family ever entered any birds to the Mains. *"There was lots of farmers and country people used to breed and rear fighting cocks. They used to put them in coops away from the farm, and rear them like pheasants. There was a good demand for good fighting cocks here in West Cumberland. They had their own secret buyers. This was a hush, hush trade. Miners, quarrymen and dealers used to go in for this fighting cock game. West Cumberland was rife for these meets that were always held in secret. My people knew the men who organised the secret meets, although we were never actually involved in this kind of sport. We were interested in road racing for side bets, and trotting one horse against the other over different types of field and moor. People were always looking for something for a gamble to try and turn it into profit."*

Another sporting activity with which John Townsley's forebears were involved, was bare knuckle fighting. *"Some of our relations used to come down from Scotland every summer, and they would camp in one of our fields. There was one family called Winter, and Jimmy Winter was a bare knuckle fighter."* Jimmy was a big powerful man, who was always keen to throw out a challenge to other travellers, or country men that were game enough, or foolish enough to take him on for side bets.

"Winner take all." was Jimmy's promise.

"He would fight for anything; horse tackle, horses, carts or anything appertaining to travellers." Prize goods were as useful to Jimmy as any money that he won, for as a dealing man he knew he could always sell his winnings and turn them into hard cash.

Dangerous Jimmy Winter was recognised as a born street fighter. He was known

Tales of a Lakeland Gypsy

as "Danger" for short. He had learned to fight the hard way on the streets of Glasgow, where no Queensberry rules governed the ferocious punishment that one fighter meted out to another. Jimmy's fights were usually only brought to an end when one man, invariably Jimmy, knocked his opponent senseless. Verdicts on points were unknown. The bare knuckle fighters fought to the finish, when one of the contestants was dragged away, bleeding and broken. The victor might also be bleeding, but his spirits were high and his pain ignored in the delight and satisfaction of claiming the winnings.

"Jimmy Winter would fight anyone. He would travel miles by road to have a fight". These travels took him all over the north of England into the violence of the fairground booths, and the hastily arranged fights in stable yards, or in the open fields. Jimmy's wife Mary "handed" him; she was the second in his corner, and enthusiastically screamed her vocal encouragement in her husband's quest for a win. John Townsley described her as a queer handful who was no mean fighter herself. *"She could PAGER [fight], and BUDICK [throw] off either hip, and she feared no one. The Gypsies in the country were scared of Mary Winter."*

Jimmy Winter was certainly not a man to be trifled with. He would swagger into a pub full of travellers or miners, eye up the potential opposition, and then throw out his challenge. There was usually someone rash enough to take him on. Jimmy took on all comers, their size and weight was immaterial to him; it was the prize that counted. Many a man, having called in the pub for a drink before taking his freshly collected pay packet home, found himself relieved of his week's wages when he was foolish enough to be drawn into a fight with Jimmy Winter. Jimmy had no qualms about fighting a man with the pay packet as the prize.

Although many of Jimmy's fights were spontaneous affairs, other bouts of bare knuckle fighting were arranged at secret locations. They took place at many different venues throughout the county, although Abbeytown, Dearham, High Harrington, Appleby, Penrith, Whitehaven and many of the mining villages had their regular fights. Word was spread discreetly, but sufficiently so to ensure that there was always an eager, jostling, noisy, supporting crowd to urge the fighters on in the hope of winning a bet. *"There was always a man to take the bets. The Galloping Horse at Harrington was a meeting place for fighting men. The fights took place in the yard. It was surrounded by a white washed wall. The men that came to the fights stayed in the stables, but took their food and drinks in the pub. There used to be Irishmen putting up in the stables with their geese to sell. They had come off the boats at Whitehaven. They used to drive the geese from place to place on the roads."*

Some of these Irishmen, who were confident in their own ability of being able to look after themselves, and with a reputation for being hard men, would willingly respond to Jimmy Winter's challenge. It was usually only a short while before they found that the strong ale of a Cumbrian pub was a good anaesthetic for the beatings they received.

Another fighting man that just remains in John's memory, was *"an old, old man that used to come down our lane. He was a large man, all of six feet four inches and*

59

Tales of a Lakeland Gypsy

around eighteen stone." This was Jont Edgar. In his prime, Jont had been a powerful fighting man. *"He dealt in fighting cocks, racing and lurcher dogs. He used to attend all the meets whether it was for bare knuckle fighting, racing dogs, or coursing hares."* One of Jont's favourite tricks when he entered a pub, or found himself among a crowd of travellers, was to throw his hat in the air and issue his own challenge to the man on whom it landed. *"I will fight any man it fits, or otherwise."* he would shout. Jont could make a lot of money by successfully fighting for side bets. John Townsley recalls being told by his Elders that Jont could really MARR, [fight], when he was a young man. *"They fought all the time down in Low Harrington where the fishermen, dockers, seamen and miners used to drink."*

John's own experience of fighting was gained from attending boxing matches that were held in the town of Workington, but these had the added sophistication that the fighters actually wore boxing gloves. The fights took place on the Cloffocks, an open area of land on the outskirts of the town. *"There was always a large following of travellers and Gypsies. Shocker Bowman and his brother used to fight at that time. Shocker was a good 'un; he went the full distance with the legendary Jock McAvoy who was a champion. They fought for a few pounds in those days. There was some good Gypsy lads boxing all over the north of England. My family used to do deals for horses and tackle at these meets, it was good for trade and business."*

The Cloffocks was used as a traditional camping ground by travellers and fair folk. In recent years, modern requirements of civic administration and demands for car parking have taken their toll of the open space which is now greatly reduced in size. The Cloffocks are bounded on one side by the river Derwent, a fast flowing river that rises high in the Lake District mountains. It enters the sea at Workington and has a long established reputation for being one of the finest salmon rivers in the country. Even today, it provides the salmon poacher, if not the legitimately licensed angler, with a rich harvest of the migratory fish. John recalled how he had been told by his Elders of the poaching that went on in West Cumberland, which in his opinion has always had a reputation as being a hotbed of poachers. A Gypsy poacher in West Cumberland is reputed to have had a violent encounter with a bailiff, with disastrous results for the latter.

> *"The Gypsy poacher said,*
> *He came at me like a lion,*
> *And me, my life to save,*
> *I struck the blow, that laid him low,*
> *And now he's in his grave."*

"In the 1920's and 1930's when times were hard, nearly all the men who lived and worked along the river were poachers to a certain extent. Some just got one to take home for their family, others, especially those who lived or worked in the dock areas, caught large amounts of fish while the season was on. It was the thing to do in those days. Even the bailiffs would turn a blind eye; some of them were poaching fish for themselves."

In John's opinion, poachers of that earlier generation were looked up to and

Tales of a Lakeland Gypsy

admired by the village people. *"It had been going on for generations. In the small villages along the Derwent and the Marron, they used to wait for the fish to start running. It was as if they were waiting for the harvest to begin. When there was a dry period of weather, the fish would queue up in the dock and the lower reaches of the river, waiting for the rain, and a rise in the water level so they could move upstream."*

By its very nature, the adult salmon is impelled to swim upstream by its innate urge to return from its travels in the oceans of the world, to seek out the river system in which it was born. Once the creature manages to sense the estuary where the fresh water of its river birthplace mingles with salt water of the sea, it homes to its native stream. The powerful breeding urge impels the fish to strive to reach the shallow, gravel bottomed spawning beds in the upper reaches of the rivers. To make this journey, the salmon has to overcome the natural predators of larger fish, marine mammals and fish eating birds before they run the gauntlet of the rod and line anglers, as well as the more direct attacks of the poachers.

"The old ones used to say, 'Ribton Hall, where Sunday never calls, Every day is just the same.' Poaching was a way of life, and everybody accepted it as such."

But changing times have brought changing methods, and modern day poachers have adopted different ways. *"A new generation of salmon poachers started netting the river at night, even when it was in flood. They were not content with an odd fish, for them poaching is a business. They had wet suits, and the team I knew had knowledge of where the bailiffs would be on certain nights. They were on the take. These boys would catch up to a ton or thirty hundredweight of fish. They would load it into a van in steel boxes that did not let the water seep out, for that is a tell tale sign. It was driven into the northern counties to be sold that same day."*

Taking out such large quantities of fish has, over the years, reduced the natural regeneration of the species, for the numbers of fish that reach the spawning beds are greatly decreased. But with the introduction and reliability of improved technology and mechanisation on the part of the National Rivers Authority, allied to an increasingly efficient organisation of policing the rivers by their water bailiffs, or "beck watchers" as they are locally known, the poachers are coming under increasing pressure.

"But the fish are not there in any great number now." was John's comment.

The illegal taking of salmon was not the only form of poaching with which John Townsley's family were familiar. Rabbits, pheasants and deer all found their way on to their business carts to be sold among the scattered West Cumbrian communities. John added that West Cumberland has always been a place for game poaching; hares, pheasants, partridges and deer were all hunted with great enthusiasm and skill. *"In the days of the eighteen hundreds, right up to the 1930's, town people, as well as country people kept ferrets, lurchers and nets for netting rabbits. But it was hardly known for anyone to be up at court for poaching. It was the done thing; if you kept off the lordy of the manor's land, you were usually alright. If a farmer caught you, you just gave him a couple of rabbits or pheasants and that was the end of it. No one bothered; many of the local poachers gave the farmer a hand at harvest time."*

Tales of a Lakeland Gypsy

John personally knew a number of local poachers, some of whom he described as "hard cases". *"I knew some poachers who carried shotguns, broken into bits, in their poachers' pockets. Some of these were desperate men, and nobody brushed with these fellas. In the twenties and thirties, people were starving, and poaching was a way of getting something to eat, or to make some money by what they caught. It was understood that they poached, and there was people to buy."*

As stretches of river and land were bought up by syndicates restricted to private fishing and shooting, it was essential that their gamekeepers did their job sufficiently well to ensure that there were plenty of fish in the river and game on the land for their paymasters to enjoy a successful day's sport.

"But the poachers knew that the gamekeepers had to sleep, and that was the time they struck. They knew he could not be everywhere at once. They used to go and clean up every fat pheasant in the woods. They used lamps to dazzle the animals and a stick to bop them."

John explained that a cart or van was always waiting nearby to be loaded up with the catch, to be delivered to hotels and restaurants in the area. *"It was cash on the nail and no questions asked."*

In some parts of Cumbria where rough wooded ground formed part of a farmer's holding, but lay unmanaged and neglected, deer and rabbit took advantage of the cover it afforded and became plentiful. *"When it was like that, the deer started to really multiply, so a landowner would get in touch with a dog man, or a poacher to go and thin them out. Some of these landowners who were in business were BENT themselves. So the Boys would start cleaning out the stock legally. At night, they strayed onto other land, and cleaned that out first, leaving the job they were asked to do till last. That gave them the perfect alibi if they were questioned. All they had to say was we have permission off Mr --, and these are deer off his land."*

John can remember visiting some of these Boys in the old buildings where they kept their dogs. *"They had so many deer carcasses hanging up it was like an abattoir."*

Many of the deer were pulled down by hunting dogs, and the Family always had these animals available for sale, as well as those that were used for hare coursing. Modern day pressure of opinion is trying to have this field sport banned, although it is still legitimately carried out under strict controls of Field Sports organisations.

Coursing is one of the oldest of field sports indicated in the records that date back to Roman times. *"The true sportsman does not take out his dogs to destroy hares, but for the sake of the course and the contest between dogs and the hares, and is glad if the hares escape."* Those words are attributed to a Roman named Arrian, who wrote them in 116 AD. In modern times, all legitimate coursing which is carried out under National Coursing Club rules, takes place in the open country where the odds are in favour of the hare escaping. *"The object of coursing under National Coursing Club rules is to test greyhounds, not kill hares."* ["This is Coursing" a leaflet published by the National Coursing Club, the official body which has regulated the sport for 150 years.]

In a legally managed course, two dogs compete against each other to chase the

Tales of a Lakeland Gypsy

hare. The dogs are usually greyhounds, although other breeds such as whippets, salukis and lurchers are sometimes loosed on the "course". The technical term for releasing the dog is "slipped", and conjures up memories of Shakespeare's words in Henry V when he likened the English soldiers, eager to get to grips with the French, as "greyhounds straining at the slips".

At the start, the dogs are held by the "slipper". If he judges that the hare, which has previously been "put up" into the coursing ground, is fit enough to escape, then the dogs are released. This only occurs when the hare has a start of at least 80 yards, a practice recommended by the National Coursing Club. An average course lasts about half to three quarters of a minute during which time a greyhound can cover almost 600 yards. The hare, with its smaller size and lower centre of gravity, is a more agile creature than the bigger and heavier dogs, and it is claimed by the National Coursing Club that seven out of eight hares that are coursed, actually make their escape. A further claim is made that research which was undertaken for the RSPCA, shows that the flight of a hare is a *"natural, instinctive and routine response to danger."* Once the hare has escaped, the dogs are called off, and that particular course should come to an end.

Coursing as John Townsley's Family knew it was not governed by the rules of the National Coursing Club, which since 1914 has banned coursing on enclosed land. Many of the meets with which the Townsleys and the Lowthers were involved were impromptu and often clandestine arrangements, which created the opportunity for money to be made with side bets. *"We used to do hare coursing on the moors. Fields were alive with hares years ago. I have seen a field lifting in one movement with hares. There used to be one meet held on either Schoose Farm or Hunday Farm land. Hares were bred there, and were looked after by the game keepers."*

Another of the country pursuits that is illegal, yet still goes on today, is the trapping and caging of wild bred birds. Many travelling Gypsies keep small birds confined in small wooden cages made of dowelling, or wicker weave. They are not always content however to merely enjoy the companionable song of a canary, or the chattering budgerigar. Travellers, with their love of bright things appreciate the variety of colour found in the plumage of such birds as linnets, greenfinches and goldfinches. At Gypsy gatherings, wild song birds are exhibited outside their owner's wagon, while others are openly offered for sale. The display of colour and song is there to catch the interest, and the pocket of bird fanciers among the FLATTIES.

John Townsley recalled the illegal, but still practised method by which these birds were caught. *"There was also country men who used to breed and trap rare birds. They used to catch them with bird lime,* [an illegal practise of smearing a sticky substance onto twigs.], *sometimes they would have a decoy bird sing in a small cage nearby. These were sold to dealers in towns and cities. It has always gone on in West Cumberland."* As present court records show, it still continues today.

Dodgy dealing was part of John Townsley's upbringing. *"The COUGERS or the FLATTIES just stood no chance when they came up against our family who were masters of dealing, but I suppose country ANTLE were not like us. We were doing it for*

Tales of a Lakeland Gypsy

our business and livelihood, but they always got a fair deal. It's life itself when you take something to trade in for something better. You had to be versatile. If one trick didn't work, then you had to try another. If it didn't work for one, there was always plenty of the family to try something else. We were heavily handed in terms of numbers." Some of the early advice John was given stood him in good stead in his own business dealings in later life. He was taught never to speak back to anyone, never to argue, or to offend people, but more importantly, trust nobody until you know better, *"for by hook and by crook they will all try to get the better of you in any dealing. Think before dealing."*

The Elders passed on tricks that they had successfully employed from years back. One concerned the weighing in of a cart before collecting bones, NATTLERS, rags and woollens in big proven bags. When going to do business, a dealer is usually required to have his vehicle checked for weight when it is both empty and full. One Townsley trick was to drive the cart on to a weighbridge at a factory or slaughterhouse, with a heap of bags loosely covering the bottom of the cart. Unbeknown to the weighman, a small member of the family was secreted inside one of the bags, only to later emerge from his hiding place and help with the loading once the weight of the empty cart had been recorded. In later years when the Family were dealing in scrap metal that they bought from factories and works, a similar ploy was used on the weighbridge when the weighmen would accept money on the side for working the following fiddle. *"They would say bring a dodgy couple of old spare wheels and some bags of sand in the bottom of the lorry before you get on the weigh bridge. We'll get rid of them for you on the night shift."* The extra weight allowance for the discarded rubbish was made up in top quality metal, for which the weighmen were paid a sum of money "on the side."

A popular form of gambling was tossing for a bet, this was an activity that John continued through to the time when he had his own yard. *"Gypsy people would say, do you want to toss? I used to toss dealer people regularly. They would say, I'll toss for twenty or thirty pounds. Some would say double or quits. My yard was noted for never turning down anyone who wanted to toss the coin."*

Chapter Seven

THE COUNTRY LIFE

A travelling Gypsy's way of life is inevitably linked to the countryside, for that environment provides many of life's basic requirements. It can offer natural cover for shelter, fuel for heating and cooking, and food from the roots, berries, fish and animals that are there to be taken, legally or illegally by those who have sufficient knowledge and skill to do so.

Although John Townsley was never a travelling Gypsy in the accepted sense of the word, his affinity for the countryside and the rewards that it brought are still deeply rooted within him. Part of his heritage lies in the tales and knowledge passed down to him by the Elders of the Family about their travelling way of life. Where it was possible to adapt these for himself, then they became incorporated into John's way of life.

But he still holds a nostalgia for the old ways. *"What a good life in the old days! A good horse and cart and rowdy, or sovereigns in your pocket, and tackle to hawk or buy whatever came up on your countrified travels. A good home and family fed on good SCRAN which you MANGED for off farmers. People lived on dealing, and you lived or hungered by that way. You could face up to anybody for you looked the part. A good outfit and LUVRE in your SKY, what more could a man want."*

When John was a young boy in the 1920's he was aware that even then the numbers of true travelling Gypsies were on the decline. *"When I was a boy, you could count travellers round the countryside on the fingers of one hand, but today, all sorts of FLATTIES want to be travellers."*

He dismisses many of the modern day travellers as being far from the genuine article. *"Most of them are not connected in any way to the true Gypsy or travelling people. They are didecoys, misfits, drop outs, dyke back people, who know their way to the PANCRACK office. My people never wanted to be anything other than what they were, white faced Gypsies who kept their feet firmly on the ground and worked for theirselves. I think I am very fortunate to have seen part of the way of life in the old days."*

The Cumbrian countryside, and its people have gone through a devastating period of change during the years of the 20th century. Native bred Cumbrians have left their home villages and valleys to seek work elsewhere; while an influx of people from outside the county has forced property prices beyond the reach of many local folk. The widespread ownership of motor cars has enabled the development of a commuter society in country communities. In some parts of Cumbria, village life has all but died as farms and cottages have been taken over to be converted to holiday homes with its transient population.

Tales of a Lakeland Gypsy

The countryside itself has changed in response to the requirements of modern day farming techniques, and the need for farmers to balance a budget and comply with rules and regulations demanded by tiers of bureaucracy. Many landlords have become faceless organisations who administer their estates from afar. Some present day visitors to the Lake District, from other parts of the country or overseas, may see it as a time capsule, a quiet retreat from the hustle and bustle of city life; but this is an illusion, for along with other parts of the country, the changes have been rapid, and in some cases, devastating.

"We travelled along paths and bridleways to keep off the rough cobbled roads. They were used all the time for moving livestock in the old days. There was the cattle drover who did nothing else except driving livestock one way, and when he got to his destination he picked up another drove to take the beasts somewhere else."

The droving days had all but gone by the time John was able to appreciate the beauty and freedom that roaming the countryside can offer; but to a man who took advantage of that freedom, the changes wrought by modern day developments are obvious. *"I loved being out in the quiet countryside. Everything was so peaceful and the people were so friendly. They were always pleased to see any of the two Families wherever we went."*

John was always fascinated by the sights and smells and beauty of the countryside. *"We knew exactly what we could gather to eat, and what we could not eat, for some of the vegetation is poisonous."* He recalled his memories of the Cumbrian country-side when he was travelling with his sisters or cousins to hawk their goods in the valleys of the western lakes. It provided them with a rich harvest of food for free. *"We used to know where all the crab apple trees were. We collected them and took them home to make crab apple jelly, and gathered burnett tops to make wine. Looking back, we used to eat all kinds of growing things when going along the bye ways and the bridleways. We ate young briar shoots off the dog rose, bread and cheese from the tender hawthorn shoots. We ate the young seed pods off the wild violet and the skin off the rose hips when they were fully ripe. We sucked nectar out of some of the wild flowers."*

They collected bags full of ripe hazel-nuts, wild strawberries and raspberries; gooseberries and blackberries all according to the season. They even used to search the wet, swampy mossy ground for cranberries and spent many back bending hours picking bleaberries from the southern slopes of the fells. From these wild fruits, the women folk made jam or wine. The white elderflowers were plucked for making "champagne", and mushrooms were gathered from the fields enriched by goodly helpings of horse manure. *"I can remember fields being white with mushrooms in the early morning; we collected them by the basketfull. We also used to dig up "devils bread" in the grazing fields and meadows. We called them hawk nuts or pig nuts. The streams and rivers were alive with salmon, while up on the fells near the clear fresh springs, was lovely fresh water cress. We used to hear the corn crake making calls to its mate, and at the right time of year, we collected peewit and partridge eggs to sell to hotels."*

Tales of a Lakeland Gypsy

John conjured up memories of farmers working in the fields, where their rate of work was governed by the slow steady progress of their team of horses, as they tilled the ground or turned the hay. Some of these farm workers used to set their time of day by the hour at which one of the Townsley carts sped by, especially when it was one of the girls that was driving.

"Farmers used to stop working in the fields to see them go by. They used to say, they are behind today, they will be trying to catch up. There was the smell and freshness of it all, especially after a heavy shower, and then in the heat, you could almost sense the crops and the plants in the hedgerow growing in front of you. You could drive through narrow lanes, and along bridleways, linking shortcuts from one village to another."

In John's opinion, the variety and quantity of wildlife and wildflowers in the countryside, were more numerous than they are today. *"Rabbits and hares were everywhere, and snipe used to fly up from the wet, rushy marshy ground. The young boys in the Families used to roam through the bluebell and cowslip woods. You could drink water from any of the fast running streams; they used to sparkle. Monkey flowers grew with marsh marigolds round the horse troughs that were set at the side of the road. These places were always wet, and wild birds used to come there to drink."*

One of John's summertime jobs was to go up on to the moors to check the horses, the mares and foals that were grazing there. *"We cut the grass on the road side verges to make hay to feed them in the winter. The different seasons meant money to Gypsies and travelling folk. My people used to gather foxgloves and kingcups and other herbs to make medicines. They were never short of vegetarian food for there were nuts and berries to gather. They knew where they grew in profusion."*

John appreciated the slower pace of life that the country life-style demanded. *"It was a slower life, yes, but it was the pace you set to visit farms, and other people adapted to it. They knew when to expect you. It didn't matter how long it took you to get there. It gave you the chance to enjoy the scenery and view the nature that was in the different landscapes."* Philosophically, John feels that people of today have missed out in not experiencing that slower life style. *"It was not how much money you had. People were not jealous; most were content with what they had."* He likened that way of life to the style that is followed by some of the Armenian settlers in the USA, where even today, their agricultural practices are governed by the use of genuine horse power.

As the Families travelled through the countryside hawking their goods, they inevitably came into contact with some of the country characters. John recalled that many of the villages in his younger days had broad grass verges, or greens where travellers halted for a few days, before moving on. *"People camped everywhere in those days, wherever there was a green or a lonnin' so you always had a chance of meeting up with travellers for a crack, or to do a deal."* There were also those who practised a more sedentary, if somewhat unusual life style.

"My father used to do business with one old woman who dressed up like a man. Her name was Maggie Midge and she lived off Wright Green, Kidburngill, Lamplugh.

Tales of a Lakeland Gypsy

She worked with the horses at Dean Moor drift mines. Her job was hauling the coal from the drift to the depot near the road. She pulled the coal wagons with her own horses, day in, day out, every day and in all sorts of weather. The majority of this coal was sold for household purposes.

Maggie Midge bought harness, flat carts and traps off my dad for private driving purposes, and for travelling round the shops and farms. She was a hard woman, the weather didn't bother her, and when she wanted to replace or exchange a horse, she got onto my dad. She never dealt with anyone else."

The railway line from Bridgefoot, near Workington, to Rowrah and Cleator Moor ran past the home of Maggie Midge. It was called the Marron line, taking its name from the river whose course it followed, and along with other small but long forgotten railway lines, carried passengers and goods and provided routes of access all over the county. One of the most famous and scenic was the Cockermouth, Keswick and Penrith railway that connected the west coast of Cumbria with the main line trains. Much of the route of this attractive line has now been overlaid by the asphalt of the A66.

When John is driving along the modern roads, memories come flooding back to him. *"Often now when out in the car, I can see our people watering the horses out of the stone troughs set in the road sides. I can picture it just as it was, and I can recall over and over again in my mind's eye, the faces of some of the old country people who lived on the farms and who dealt with us."*

One of those faces belonged to an old farmer, John Potter. *"He was a farmer and a milkman who lived in sweet Ennerdale. He always had a great beard. He would wait for us at a given point to catch us for fish and herring. He lived down a long, bad farm lane and he always bought his horses for the milk round, and taking him to market, from my dad."*

Many of the farms that John visited on his rounds were small, and just worked by the family. For the farmers who could afford to hire extra labour, they took on lads and lasses from the hiring fairs that were held twice a year in the nearby market towns. Anyone could join the crowd that thronged the streets, hoping to attract the attention of a prospective employer. A wage was negotiated for a six month term, with food and board thrown in. At the end of their six month term, they were free to negotiate a further contract, or return to their homes for a short break of a few days before resuming work with their employer.

"We used to pick up some of the farm workers and their portmanteaus and bring them home if they were leaving that particular farm. The men, lads and lasses would come down our lane to buy their second hand clothes for their next six months of work on the land and farm service."

Some of the country characters the Family encountered were somewhat intimidating. One of these was sometimes referred to as the Lion Tamer. *"My brother Charlie was working the high country one day; that's Arlecdon, Lamplugh and beyond to Ennerdale. He saw this woman running down the road towards him shouting for help. It was pouring down with rain, and bitterly cold for it was winter time. The woman*

Tales of a Lakeland Gypsy

wore no coat ; she only had a pinafore on top of her dress, and clogs on her feet. As she got near, she shouted Charlie save me, he's coming after me." She had run several miles over rough moorland to escape from her husband, who had a reputation for being something of a wild man. John explained that this couple were FLATTIES who had a large family and managed to scrape a living during the hard times, by selling firewood from their horse turnout.

The Townsleys knew the family through dealing and trading with them. *"Charlie said, Jump into the trap, lay down in the well and I'll cover you up with a couple of old coats. She told Charlie that she had not been working hard enough to satisfy her husband; her job was to saw up the firewood, and bag it. There were a number of lads in her family, but none of them dare challenge their father. Charlie said, he won't touch me, I am afraid of no man. Charlie stood six foot three, and could jump off each leg, and kick the eye out of a fly."*

With the woman well hidden in the trap, Charlie Townsley drove on to complete his rounds. He hadn't gone far when he met the husband coming hell for leather over the brow of the hill.

"Have you seen out of the wife, Charlie?"
"Yes" said Charlie, "she has taken the Gilgarran road".
"I'll get her" he said."

and off he went in the opposite direction, driving his horse at a mad gallop. Charlie dropped the woman off at her home hoping that her husband's temper would have cooled off by the time he returned.

Members of the Townsley family also sold firewood, some of which was obtained from the woodland that surrounded a large house out in the country. *"There was this large mansion out in the country with woodlands, gardens and gardeners, grooms, horses and all sorts of horse drawn vehicles. They used to buy fish and pots from us, and also horses when they needed them. The house stood between two roads, there were two big entrances at each road, and we were given permission to go through their driveway, even when we were not calling on them. There was a large saw mill where we used to buy loads and loads of sawn up logs to sell in the towns. In the winter time, we went there regularly with a four wheeled dray to buy the wood and take it to Harrington. The Family always had two carts doing the rounds and selling the wood."*

When the internal combustion engine made its presence known in the form of model T Fords, and Lagondas, the Family bought some to use in their business, as they realised that this form of transport would enable them to get further, and more rapidly into the countryside than they had been able to travel with their horses and traps. The carts and traps were still used by the girls, but the men folk took to the road in one of the old cars. The girls, however, quickly learned to drive the cars as well as they could handle the horse traps.

Learning to drive was a straightforward sort of business in those early days when the roads were quiet and, for most of the time, deserted. *"You didn't have to take a test; it was just a matter of picking it up as you went along. I used to get behind the steering*

Tales of a Lakeland Gypsy

wheel when I was six years old. We had bull nose Morris and Austin 12 - 4 with the bulb horn, and the gate change. You had to crank them on the starting handle, to get them to start, and watch it didn't kick back. It could sprain or even break your wrist." There was no turning of a key in an electric ignition system, and the hard work of getting the car started was probably one of the reasons that the girls preferred to stick to driving horses, even though John described some of the animals as having, *"half a ton of live muscled up energy to control."*

"I remember the cars; they had wooden spoked wheels. They had dickie seats and a hot and cold temperature gauge on the radiator cap. There was not that many travellers dealing in the Lakes and other parts of Cumberland. You could get out to these far parts, and back again in the same day with the motors. When we called on rows of terraced houses, I used to be behind the wheel. One of the boys would shout, Let the brake off John. If we were on an incline, the car would roll a few yards until I stopped it, so that we could serve some more customers."

The Family found another use for their vehicles among the country folk. After their days' work of delivering from their vehicles was completed, the boys would come back home, get washed and changed before going back out in their cars to use them as taxis. *"My cousins and my brother in law used to take sportsmen all over the county to wrestle, run and leap in the Lakeland sports. They also took men who were in the hound trailing business, and their dogs out to the trails. We used to save waste parts of fish for these men to use to feed their dogs. There was always a spare car if people wanted to hire it for anything special, then they could. Petrol was cheap, and you could buy it from nearly any country shop in a two gallon tin. It was mostly Spratts or National Benzole, and we always had a couple of cans strapped on to the running boards in case we ran out of petrol when we were out in the wilds."*

A regular stopping off place for the Family in the Lamplugh area, was at the shop of Mrs Horsley at Cross Gates. This was one of a row of cottages at the crossroads of the Cockermouth - Whitehaven road, and that which comes from Workington to cross the low lying slopes of the western fells that shelter the village and valley of Ennerdale.

"Mrs Horsley was a nice, kindly old lady. Her country shop, like all the others was full of old fashioned smells. There was various old fashioned soaps, like carbolic, herbs hanging up, camphor balls they used to put in clothes to keep the moths away. There was bacon, boiled ham and cheese on the counter waiting to be cut with the knife. She had treats for the kids like lollipops, sherbet and liquorice sticks, and when you went in or out of the door, the bell would ring behind you. There was always plenty of old fashioned crack going on there for those with time to listen. The Boys would always buy a few tins off her, as she always bought off us. She sold petrol by the tinful, and it used to stand in tins outside the shop. It was around nine pence a gallon, and there was a charge on the tin which was returnable. Mrs Horsley used to take messages at the shop for the country people who wanted to buy things off us, such as pots, or PONGO [linoleum] or do a deal. We got messages to do for her as well, like delivering things to the Knockmurton iron ore mines."

One of the first garages in the area was to be found at Cross Gates. It belonged to

70

Tales of a Lakeland Gypsy

Dick Horsley who did car repairs in his shed in those early motoring days. *"I visited the garage with my brother in law, and cousins to get small repairs done to our cars, or just to trade with him, and buy his scrap. He was quite a character, and there was another called Sydney Bruce; he was a sportsman and drove a Singer le Mans sports car. I can remember the colour; it was red."*

Cross Gates was only a short distance away from the iron ore mines of Knockmurton, and John recalled that those mines around Lamplugh were busy places, for they were the main providers of employment in the area. *"The lanes and the roads ran red when it was wet. It used to stain everything, and the miners who walked for miles to get to work were all covered in red dust."* It was for this reason that the mine workers in the nearby town of Egremont earned themselves the nickname, the Red Men of Egremont. The scars of spoil heaps and the hollows of collapsed workings are all that now remain of a once thriving industry, but as the Family travelled about the countryside, it was the horns and hooters of the quarries and mines that sounded at the end of a shift that told them the time of day.

"We could always tell the time of day by the horns and hooters of the quarries and mines that used to blow at the end of a shift; and the trains that ran on the country railways." Of more importance than time to the Family, was the fact that the mines and quarries supplied a considerable amount of scrap metal. Many of the railway embankments that carried those lines are still there to be seen, but most were closed in the thirties and their rails also sold off for scrap.

John's earliest memory of venturing into the scrap dealing business was when he accompanied his brother in law, Bill Lowther into what he called the high country of Ennerdale.

"When I was just a young lad, I was coming down this mountain track off the fell tops, with one of the men. We had on board a load of CHOREY metal. It was about two o clock in the morning. We had been to this mine, at midnight, by arrangement with the owner and manager to buy some scrap. The metal was BENT; but as far as we knew the metal was theirs, and no doubt insured. We had a thick black cob yoked into a light weight four wheeled lorry. We just got to the steepest part of the track, when the back band broke in two. We managed to pull broadside across the track to take the steep drop out of the situation."

One can imagine the scene of disarray as the scrabbling hooves of the horse sought for purchase on a loose and slippery surface, the cart tilted over, man and boy searching for the damage to the harness in the darkness of a Lakeland night; grunts and oaths as the bags of heavy metal were unloaded so that the damage could be rectified and the journey resumed before daylight.

"We had to tip some of the metals, the copper and the brass out of the bags, tie them together to make a makeshift back band. We were the best part of twenty miles and we were keeping off the roads as much as possible. We kept to the fields and bridleways and eventually got home. There was not many OWNIES [police] about in those days."

Tales of a Lakeland Gypsy

The wives of the iron ore workers, miners and dockers in the West Cumbrian towns were all good customers of the Family in their dealings of second hand clothes. That meant that some of the Family had to drive through to Whitehaven to stand on the Open Market. *"Many of the women needed old clothes for they worked at the pit top on the conveyer belts which carried the coal for sorting. The women lined alongside the belts taking out all the stone and RATTLER, so that they just left the clean coal. Others wanted some of the second hand clothes that we bought off the gentry, and this they kept for their best."*

Much of this good quality clothing was obtained when the girls went hawking to the large country houses to exchange PONGO and household goods, for second hand clothes. *"Pongo was linoleum. We used to get a van load of PONGO and sell it over a wide area. We used to sell it on to other travelling people. Sometimes they walked for miles through the countryside, carrying the rolls over their shoulders. When they knocked at doors, they stood the PONGO on end, and unrolled a few yards out flashing it off. They showed the soundness of it by banging it with the flat of their hands."* The travellers were persuasive salesmen for they were reluctant to leave a house without completing a sale. They didn't like any unnecessary journey that meant carrying the heavy rolls of lino on their shoulders.

While much of the second hand clothing trade was conducted at the weekly markets in the towns, they also did regular trade by taking the TUGGERY on their travels to remote country areas. Those country folk that had money to spare were always pleased to see the carts loaded up with Lancashire prints that were bought directly from the mill, linen imported from Ireland or the colourful Paisley silk shawls. Pots were always in great demand among the country folk, and to ensure there was always a ready supply available, the Family kept a Kendal pot cart ready stocked to go out on the road. The pots were delivered to Harrington by rail, despatched in the safety of straw packed containers directly from the manufacturers in the Potteries, China, which is loved by all travelling families, was sent up from Handley Bros, Stoke on Trent.

An essential item for which there was always a demand was the chamber pot to tuck away under a bed. Earth closets at the bottom of a garden were a reality in those days, and the convenience and improved hygiene afforded by modern day plumbing, lay ahead in the distant future. Some of the prices of the pots may seem very cheap by today's standards of household income, but when compared to a wage of a few shillings a week, they assume a proportional value.

> *Half a dozen large plates   1/-*
> *half a set of china   2/-*
> *roasting pans   3d & 6d*
> *pans with lids   6d*
> *bass matting runners for house floors   3d a piece*
> *coal, seven pence a hundredweight.*

"In most villages, or among the rows of terraced houses that lined the roads, you would always find one man who knew what was going on in the area." John referred to him as the local NARK who gleaned much of his information from gossip in the pub,

Tales of a Lakeland Gypsy

or simple hours of observation while the work was going on in the fields, or from quietly watching the world pass by, from the vantage point of a seat on a door step. The Families had these men giving them the news. *"He would say; Your Uncle Charlie's lads have just passed through with a few horses tied up behind the flat cart. On another occasion it might be; have a run up to the farm at the lonnin', he' s got some pigs and poultry to sell."*

If something was needed at an outlying farm, word would be passed through to the local "tipster" who passed on the message, *"They said if I saw you, to pass on the message they want to see you about a bit of business."*

Some of the old men who passed on this information were very knowledgeable about horses, as they had worked with them all their lives. They knew where there were good horses that were underworked. John's grandfather was told of one such horse on a grocery delivery round.

"To tell you the truth, it was flying like a bird on the wing". The elder Townsley stared at the man, and said, *" I never saw yan pen feathered let alone full flighted."*

But the Family's special tipster was an old man who lived close to a dealing family on Whillimoor. Their homes were a series of shacks, snuggled under the high field walls which afforded them some form of shelter. Whillimoor, had a reputation for the quality of its cheese, hard, tough and almost inedible, which was made from the milk of cattle that were foddered on the bleak and desolate moorland. *"We used to buy the home made Whillimoor cheese from the farmers wives; it was known as "Whillimoor Wang".*

The area, from which the cheese takes its name is swept by the winds that rage in from the nearby Irish Sea, and its higher situation lends the additional chill that exposure brings. It is an inhospitable area, where the rank and poor nature of the soil made it difficult for man and beast to scratch a living. Any additional income that these hardy folk could raise was most welcome.

"I was down at the market, and heard that horse you bought was a runaway at Carlisle", the Townsleys would be told. With this sort of information, it meant that the horse could be bought very cheaply at the buyer's price, and make a good saving.

"This is how we worked with lots of FLATS. Then he would look for some money on the side from us. But we didn't mind paying for information for in the long run, it saved us, and made us a lot of money." There was no need of the telephone, word of mouth was enough to pass on information in John Townsley's younger days.

Some of the country folk that John and his family met with in the course of a day's business showed apprehension when the hawkers drew up in their village or farm. *"When they used to see you coming, they would run and hide themselves, even though they knew you. Then when you stopped with them to sell fish, or do business they would come out and talk and buy from us. Really they were RADGE. They would come to us and hand out tea and cakes. Really they were good people with countrified RADGENESS in them. Some of them had never been off their farms even for the hirings."*

Tales of a Lakeland Gypsy

Sometimes when the members of the Family were on their rounds in the country areas, they were asked to buy some unusual items. John recalled one day that he visited a farm where the owner had recently died and the wife was left to sell off the farm. She took John to a part of the farm where sheep pens railed off an enclosure.

She said," Would you buy these?"

John looked around, but apart from the rails of the pens, he could see nothing but muck.

She said, "Take this spade and clean the top off the ground."

Underneath, he found old fashioned stone troughs in all sorts of sizes that had been inverted and fitted together to create the floor of the sheep pens. *"There was sixty three stone troughs, all upside down. I was given the chance to buy them, but when I went back, the son had sold them all."*

Stone troughs, where animals could be watered, were once a common sight along the roads and by ways, but in many Cumbrian villages where the Townsley's traded, the water supply for the village community was the village pump. *"They were made of lead and iron. People used to gather round the pump for a crack while they were waiting to fill their buckets. Most houses had a wash house with a big wood and coal fired set pot. This was used for washing the clothes and also for making the soup."*

It was common practice among the country folk that once the fire was lit under the set pot, maximum use was made of its heating capacity. After the washing was done and the pot rinsed out, it was a simple enough matter to refill it with water, toss in a sheep's head, or some bones, stir in plenty of vegetables, stoke up the fire and let the broth simmer away. There was always plenty to supply not only the immediate family, but neighbours in the village. In these communities, it was a wise policy to ensure that the washing days were staggered by the different families so that there was a good pot of broth on the boil almost every day of the week. Many a good smell seeped from under the wash house door once the washing was done.

Many of the farms where the Family had dealings, were small establishments on land that belonged to a landlord. *"Most of them were tenant farmers, and often the buildings were very poor. Cow byres, barns and outbuildings were in very bad repair."* These farms were often on land of poor quality where the grass in the fields competed with sieves, ragwort, thistle and whin bushes. Hedges and dykes were broken down, and in John's words were *"stuffed with anything to keep the animals from straying".* The farmers walked the cattle to market when they had any to sell. There were some good landlords who were fair men that looked after the interests of their tenants in an interested and kindly manner, and almost regarded them as extensions of their own families. Others took the attitude that they owned their tenants as equally as the land that they let out. John recalled long gone conversations with a gamekeeper who was employed on a large estate.

" Sixty years ago, I knew an old gamekeeper; he was a master with remedies and health care for dogs. He and his sons had been keepers on a number of large estates throughout Cumberland. He used to tell me what went on at some of the wild parties

Tales of a Lakeland Gypsy

they had. The better MANTLE drove there in their four in hand carriages. Most of the workers lived in tied cottages and if they had any young daughters, fifteen or sixteen years old, they would be summoned to the big house for the master's pleasure. If they would not go, or submit their bodies to full sex, then the families could be thrown out of their cottages. The old gamekeeper said he had seen this happen over and over again."

While on their rounds members of the Family visited farms, and other folk that kept horses to buy horse hair. *"They would usually have it in a bag in the stables. Some people wanted it weighed so that they got paid by weight. We always carried a pair of spring stilliards for weighing things. Other people would just say guess the weight. They were all paid at a rate for a pound weight. When we got back to the yard, the hair was baled into large bundles and it was sent by rail to its destination. We also bought sheeps' wool and skins, and cow tailings, and these were also baled and sent by rail to Yorkshire. We also carried small spring balances to weigh the gold and silver that country folk wanted to sell."*

Throughout the year, each of the wild fruits had its own season and the Family would buy these from the country folk to sell on to fruiterers and greengrocers in the towns. They acted as the middleman. *"We took all kinds of berries that the country folk had picked, damsons, plums, blea berries and blackites [blackberries]. Some they would give to us to make jam."*

In the years after the first world war, when the country was trying to recover from the devastating losses to the male population, there were hard times for the farmers. *"Many of them were desperate for us to take out grazing on their land so they had some money coming in for cropping. It was good for us for we could buy the very best of hay at cheap prices. They were desperate days, they wanted the money for their goods so badly. Eggs were eighteen to twenty for a shilling [5p]; home baked bread was a penny a loaf and you could buy twenty home made cakes for a shilling. Steak and butcher's meat was very cheap and when you bought it from the country people, they usually gave you a black pudding or potted meat for nowt. You could buy a horse drawn load of hard wood logs from the sawmill for a few shillings and you could use these for yourself or sell them over again. People liked to see your money as it was so very scarce. People who didn't have a horse and cart had to walk everywhere. They used scythes to cut the hay, and even had to bring it in from the fields on a wheelbarrow with a board across the top."*

Sometimes, the struggle to earn a living in the countryside just became too much for some and they were forced to sell up what they had, *"I have seen farm sales where you could have bought the lot for a few quid"*. When things became really desperate, John recalled there was no other alternative but to seek help from the workhouse. *"These were places where destitute people used to go and they were given jobs like breaking stones for maintaining and repairing the roads, or chopping sticks. The poor used to get what was known as Parish Relief and for them, life was just an existence, but lots of people were glad of it."*

John recalled that some of the country people that he met on his rounds as a young boy had a strangeness about them. Some of these, with whom he could understand and sympathise, were the result of shell shock incurred during the first world war. But there were others, who appeared to be "moonstruck", for their strange behaviour coincided with, and seemed to be affected by, the different phases of the moon. He also came into contact with a number of country folk who followed the ways of minority religious sects. *"There was strange religious people who used to put notes, or religious texts on to tree trunks, or farm gates, and sometimes there were meetings held in the farmhouses where the farmer did the preaching."*

This was not an uncommon practice among the Cumbrian farming community, for in farms with a large family and a number of servants, it was more practicable for the farmer to conduct his own religious service in the farm house, and have his work force immediately available to carry on with their jobs, rather than lose them for a longer period of time to attend church some distance away. Another option was offered by a travelling minister who used to journey from farm to farm on the circuit horse, or driving the circuit trap to conduct services at the farm.

"There was all kinds of religions and denominations that included Band of Hope, Rechabites, Salvation Army, Plymouth Brethren, several kind of non conformists as well as Church of England and the Roman Catholic Churches. I think people in those days were more God fearing than they are now."

Some of the old dealers and travellers also had strange ways and strange ideas, while many of them were very superstitious. Some of them felt so strongly about omens that they wouldn't leave their homes for a day's work if something upset them. *"They didn't like to see various things cross their paths, especially if they were on their way to go hawking or calling in the morning. They would turn round and go back home, and say, there's no luck today. Some of the omens were handed down through generations and represented bad luck."*

Near to John's home in Harrington was another old character that he remembered.

"There was an old housewife in Harrington who was a real old character. Her name was Old Rachel. She had a weakness for drink. She would come down our lane looking for empty beer bottles and siphons to take back to the pub to get the deposit back to buy drink. She used to say, If I can just get a snecklifter, I'll be alright. She used to spend the night in the back room with the landlady. She was harmless and a good old woman. One night in the depth of winter, she got really drunk. She could hardly stand, and was unable to walk home on her own. So two men put her in a wheelbarrow and wheeled her down home. They knocked at the door, and walked away leaving her in the barrow."

Unfortunately, Rachel's husband, although he was in the house, had failed to hear the knocking on the door and was unaware of his wife sleeping away outside. There she remained all night. *"When he opened the back door the next morning, there she was; frozen to death in the barrow."*

John used to meet other dealers while on his rounds, some of these were

Tales of a Lakeland Gypsy

packmen, who carried their wares in a bundle either on the back or under the arm. They sold small items such as cottons, needles, ribbons, buttons, elastic, that were essential to the smooth running of everyday life on the farm. Packmen had their regular rounds in the Lake District where they visited remote hamlets and isolated farms. They were always made welcome by the farmers wife with a bite to eat and a drink to help them on their way. They were no competition to the members of the Family who were able to carry a larger and wider range of goods in their carts. Packmen were a hardy breed. They walked the roads and lanes, and crossed the fells whatever the weather. It is said that one packwoman died when descending Rossett Gill into Langdale and is reputed to be buried in a lonely spot on the fell side.

John's earliest recollection of meeting one of these packmen. was when he was returning home with his eldest sister Lizzie driving the trap. *"We had just crested the top of Dean Moor in black darkness; not a thing moved on the road. Then in the light of the candle lamps we saw a figure of a man step out into the road. It was an old dealing man on his way out of Lamplugh. He was called Billy Varey. He had a pack under his arm with his hawking tackle in it. He used to walk fifteen to twenty miles a day calling on farms. I was just a boy then, it was dark, but my sister recognised this tall man in the middle of the road. We could just make him out by the light of the trap lamps."*

He shouted, *"Is that you Lizzie?"*

"Is that you Billy Varey" she said.

"Yes, it's me" he replied.

"You're late on the road tonight" said Lizzie *"Jump in the trap and pull that old coat round you. We won't be long till we're dropping you off."*

They sped off over the dark moorland roads, by the faint light of the lamps and the sharp clatter of hooves on the road. When Billy was dropped off some six miles later, he paused to say,

"Lizzie, that's some GALLOWAY, and you are the best driver of a road horse I have ever ridden beside", he told her before leaving them to make his way back to the Cloffocks on the outskirts of Workington, where his family were camping.

The countryside that John knew now exists only in his memory. *"Some of the small copses and woodlands where we used to play as small children have disappeared. They've been bulldozed by farmers' tractors to clear the ground for grazing or cropping."*

77

*Four man power equals one horse power when
breaking in a new horse, Lorton 1915.*

Parade of horse drawn vehicles, June 25th 1914, Workington.

Chapter Eight

LIFE WITH THE HORSES

John Townsley was born towards the end of an era when the horse was essential to the pursuit of the everyday way of life, both in the town and the country. Even now, after he has had many years of experience with some of the finest cars and lorries that were available to him, John very much appreciates the fact that he lived through the last twenty years of the horse and cart days.

"I would never have liked to have missed them. If you like, I have seen the old, and the new sides of life. It was slower in the old days, but I think they were happier times. I have seen me, when a boy, away with my sister selling fish in the high country and over the fells to outlandish hamlets. We were away by six in the morning with the lamps lit, always with a good road hack between the shafts, and away till six o clock at night. We had some great horses; they were in their element when in the shafts. We always carried a whip; but it was very rare that they were used. We just used to speak to the good hacks, they knew the road and were always ready to go at any time. When you had a real good hack in the shafts, distance was nothing but a pleasure. Anything other than a good horse between the shafts was hard on the driver, and it made the day seem longer and even the road home at night seemed longer."

To the Townsley families, having horses in their fields was like having money in the bank. In many ways it was better from the Family's point of view, for the realisation of their capital was readily available. There was always someone wanting to buy a horse. The long established traditions of the Townsley and Lowther families as horse dealers ensured that they were able to supply the demands of an ever present market. Advertisements such as the one below were a familiar sight in the local press.

"FOR SALE - ONE WELSH COB MARE,
FOURTEEN. TWO HANDS. LIVER CHESTNUT.
FOUR WHITE SOCKS, FLAXEN MANE AND TAIL.
NO DEALERS NEED APPLY."
Townsley, The Lonning High Harrington."

"In the old days, trading was more than a way of life, it was life itself. There was no other way. There was so little to do, but trade. Horse trade seemed to be the thing, because there was a demand at all times for various types of good work horses, heavy types, and of course, good road horses. It seemed to be the more horses you had, or the more horses you traded, that was a sign of wealth. Even the men who worked with horses on the farms got more pay than the average none skilled worker. They seemed to be looked up to by the farmers."

John recalled driving out into the country with some of the Townsley men in the 1920's; *"We took six or seven haltered horses behind the traps, and by the end of the*

79

Tales of a Lakeland Gypsy

day they had been sold and we had bought twenty young Clydesdales to be broken and sold for the heavy carting jobs."

The Townsleys used to attend the Wigton Horse Sales every year, where they would take already broken animals that were easy to handle, and also buy young, unbroken horses fresh from the fell. The Wigton sales were established in the Cumbrian market town in 1890, and they still continue on a twice yearly basis through to the present date. When the great shire horses were in demand for working the land, it was necessary to spread the sales over three days, for then, almost 1000 Clydesdales were sold on the first two days, while the road and riding horses were sold on the third day. In the 1920's, as much as 200 pounds would change hands for a good Clydesdale mare.

Many of the horses that the Townsleys sent to Wigton for the sales were driven there along the narrow West Cumbrian roads that were as yet uncluttered by vehicular traffic. It was a leisurely procession through the agricultural country side. As they neared the small market town, they were joined by others, who also did the journey "on hoof" from places that were within a couple of days walk of Wigton. Those who had to make the journey from further afield arrived by rail. Wigton was a busy little station which was tidily kept by the stationmaster and his staff of porters and signalmen, where the cheerful flower beds brightened up the grey red expanse of platform slabs. Once the horses had been unloaded from the confines of the wooden railway wagons, the streets of the small town clattered to the ringing of hoofs and loud shouts of men, as the animals were driven towards the iron railed pens of the auction yards.

It was regarded by many, that the horse sales of Wigton and Lanark were the two most prestigious venues in the country, for the animals offered for sale were of a high quality. It was the practise at Wigton, that before any selling began, the heavy horses were examined and judged to select the finest in the sale. To have a horse that was chosen as champion at Wigton, was a tremendous accolade for its owner.

But Wigton was not the Family's favourite dealing place; that honour was reserved for Rosley fair, one of about thirty such fairs that were held throughout the county of Cumberland in the mid eighteenth and early nineteenth centuries.

The small village of Rosley is only a few miles from Wigton, and was an equally suitable place for dealers to meet up from all over the country. *"It was the most important for my people. They used to get people coming from over the Border to buy horses from the Townsleys who originated in Scotland. Yes Rosley Fair was the Family's favourite. Once a fortnight, everybody landed up there; vagabonds, thieves, losers, drunks, cardsharks, pickpockets, the lot. Five hundred horses would be sold there in a day, along with hundreds of black cattle. The old ones said that everything was sold from all sorts of livestock, geese, poultry, running dogs like lurcher dogs, as well as cloth, food and footwear. There was always horse racing and challengers for so many sovereigns in side bets. Our people used to say, let other lasses go to the Fair, but our lasses stay at home. The Elders said the fiddlers and their music were in great demand at the nearby inn, or public house."*

Tales of a Lakeland Gypsy

The Fair was reputed to have been a popular target for cattle stealing during the days of the cross Border raiding parties, while the travellers to the Fair provided rich pickings to footpads and highwaymen. Rosley Fair was held on the fringe of the John Peel hunting country, on the road between Wigton and Penrith. The famous huntsman used to attend on a regular basis and it is reputed that he was enjoying himself at Rosley Fair on a day that his wife was due to give birth to one of their children. Much to the disgust of his mother in law, Peel preferred to spend the day among his hunting and farming companions, rather than stay at home to await the arrival of his child. *"I have been told by my Elders that they did business with John Peel at Rosley fair."* The other major horse fairs where there was money to be made in horse dealing were at Appleby and Brough Hill. *"It was a must for the breed, to go to those places to sell horses, harness, horse drawn vehicles and lurcher dogs."*

The members of the Townsley families were so numerous that they could afford to have some of their men folk trading and dealing at Fairs as far away as Scotland. *"They used to drive their horses loose from Harrington to these distant Fairs and there was always plenty of helpers to give them a hand."*

Over the years, the different generations of the Townsley and Lowther families acquired many horses from these and other fairs and sales. Along with those bought from Wales and Ireland, they provided the Family with their working and dealing stock. John Townsley has the memory of the fields that belonged to his Elders being so full of horses, that the ground appeared to be black.

Every Sunday was a busy day for horse trading down the Townsleys' lane. *"The Boys were always early risers, and they had a saying that one hour in the morning is worth two in the afternoon. In other words, if you had made money before dinner, you were not chasing it in the afternoon."*

The horses were washed, and meticulously groomed until their coats gleamed. Their manes were brushed, and sometimes their tails were plaited. *"It was always the road horses that got the special treatment. They were groomed until you could see yourself through the shine of their coats."* They were then ready for inspection by the visitors to the yard, who came, either to buy a horse for the first time, or to upgrade their existing animal in much the same way as modern day motorists part exchange their car for a more efficient model. *"All the horses for sale were tied up by the wall, washed and polished up to catch the eye. Those that came were all out to get a better driving horse than the next man."*

John explained that there was a lot of rivalry between the country gentlemen who kept coming back to the lane for a better turnout, or a better horse. *"There was a local man who owned farms, and he was also an auctioneer, and if he saw someone with a better turnout than him, he would be down the lane to see the lads about getting him something better."* Today's image of one upmanship seems to have changed little during the passing years of the twentieth century.

There was also a good selection of different types of carts and traps that were for sale. These were on display, along with various items of appropriate harness and tackle. There was even a heavy dray that was kept for showing off the paces and style of Clydesdale horses to brewers or timber merchants, who needed the power of heavy horses for making their deliveries. John recalled what it was like down the lane on a Sunday. *"They were all waiting for the customers; farmers, traders or dealers. There was always an open table with home made cakes, bread and jam, roast beef. This was for those who bought or swapped with the family. There was always plenty going on. People also knew that whatever they had to sell, they could always trade it, or sell it down the lane. My people just lived for business and trade. They got enjoyment doing deals."*

Among the variety of harness that the Family had for sale, were new items that were bought in from manufacturers in Walsall. These were delivered to the nearby railway station. For those customers, who were unable, or unwilling to pay the higher prices that were asked for new harness, the Family could always satisfy their needs from the thriving second hand trade. Second hand tackle was bought in from both the business and farming communities, as part of the Families day to day dealings.

An essential part of the horse tackle was the whip. John Townsley explained that there were different whips for different purposes, and included those needed for driving, hunting and riding. *"In the 1800's and before, we bought a parcel or a quantity from the makers who were Crawley and Son who lived in Bedfordshire and who had a shop in Priestgate. They moved to Peterborough, and called their whips the Peterborough whips. We also bought horse whips from a factory in Germany, they were called Muller whips, and were lined so far up with leather. We also bought London whips that were specially made in this country. As a boy I used to collect the whips that came 12 in a bundle, from High Harrington railway station. We were always looking for new fashions in the goods we sold."*

To make sure that all their horse tackle was well maintained, or where necessary restored to its best possible condition, the Family used to provide board and lodgings for an itinerant saddler. In return for his keep, the old man used to spend a few days with the Family carrying out any repair or maintenance work that needed to be done to saddles and harness. *"He was an old man, who used to stay for days on end, in one of the outbuildings. He repaired the harness and the cart gear. He re-covered saddles and collars with good wearable cloth that went inside the collars and the saddles."*

While the quality of the harness and tackle was of a relatively stable nature, the same could not be said of the temperament of some of the horses for whom the tackle was designated. Some animals caused quite a few problems to their owners. A common difficulty that the local tradesmen experienced with their horses was that they became over lively. John explained that this was due to the fact that the animals were doing so little hard work that it made them difficult to control. To illustrate his point, he told of a case that concerned a Harrington milkman. *"He kept coming back to us to change his horse. It had so little work to do delivering milk locally that it got so fit it got hard to handle. With good food and so little work to do, these horses got fit and fiery. We were always happy to do an exchange, for we got a good animal back, plus BOUT money. We liked these sorts. We could make them shudder, and have them eating out of our hands after a day in the fish cart."*

Tales of a Lakeland Gypsy

He told of another milkman, who owned what John described as a real road horse, *"but he was frightened of it."* One day, through the Townsleys' information network, they heard that the horse had gone lame. *"He was just going to send it to the Mellbreak kennels, to be slaughtered for dog food for the pack of hounds. We just got there in time and bought it. Within a week, with rest and poultices, it was sound as a bell, and the lasses gave it the high country every day. What a sort it turned out to be. A day later, and it would have been dog meat for the fox hounds."*

"Plenty of road work" was, in John's opinion, the best cure for quieting a fiery horse, as he told of another that came into the Townsleys' hands. This horse turned out to be too much of a handful for its owner. *"Another milkman had this lovely chestnut driving horse, and he sent for my brother Charlie to see if he would buy it. When he went, they were feeding it through a partition in the stable. They were frightened to death of it. Charlie bought it, and sold the milkman another. In two days, this wild horse was yoked up, and quiet as a lamb."*

Another horse whose owner found difficulty in keeping it under control, was the means by which the children of Harrington enjoyed free helpings of ice cream. *"One summer night in the 1920's an ice cream turnout came flying down the road, and the horse and turnout went straight into some iron railings in front of some semi detached houses right against where we lived. The horse could not move as its head was jammed through the railings, and it had bent the bars. It was trapped. Our boys managed to free the horse. They took it out of the trap and also looked after the driver. One of them jumped in the ice cream cart and started giving free ice cream to all the children while the other boys took the horse out of the cart."*

The Italian driver was shaken up, but apart from the shock of finding that all his ice cream had disappeared, he was no worse. The Townsleys asked questions about the horse and expressed an interest in buying the animal, which the ice cream vendor was only too glad to sell as a runaway, there and then. *"My dad said, you must understand this horse is a runaway, and as such it's a danger on the road. You will have to take my price, alright?"*

"The horse is yours" he was told.

John described the horse as a beauty to look at. *"It was a black cob, well fed and not enough work. It got into overdrive and the GADGE could not handle it and lost control."* That same night, it was yoked into a trap and did the best part of twenty miles. That particular horse continued to work the high country for the Townsleys and never put a foot wrong. *"Many people wanted to buy her, but my father kept her and bred a couple of pedigree Welsh cobs out of her."*

Italian ice cream vendors were the targets of some of the dodgy horse dealing tricks that went on. *"We used to sell horses to the ice cream men in West Cumberland. We sold one of them his own horse back again."* John explained how it had happened. An Italian ice cream vendor had come "down the lane" to look for a new horse. His eye was taken by a smart looking black animal. He asked for the horse to be run up and down the lane to show what it could do. The demonstration met with the approval of the ice cream man, and so the deal was clinched. He took the horse away, but after a couple of days he came back down the lane with a complaint. The blackness of the horses coat that had attracted the Italian was gradually disappearing.

"The little Italian started to cry,
Who blacked the poor little horse?"

The dye that the Townsleys had used to change the appearance of the horse had started to run, as the sweat from the animal released the false pigmentation. Not recognising the animal in its new colouration as one that had previously belonged to him, the ice cream man thought he had bought a new horse. *"But it was all sorted out. He liked the horse and decided it was a good 'un so would keep it."*

Ice cream vendors were not the only the only ones to be fooled by the way the Family were able to change the appearance of horses that were bought in. *"Farmers have been known to buy their own horses back. They would come back to our yard a few days after they had sold us a horse, and buy the same one back, thinking it was a different one. All that happened was that the horse was washed, its mane cut or plaited, maybe it would be clipped out and freshly shod. You could get a horse shod with four iron shoes for three shillings. We would feed it up on some good oats and hay, and in a few days, it would look a lot better and sharper."*

There were other dodges involving dyes, which were used not only to alter the appearance of a horse, but to make it look younger than its actual age. *"That used to be an old dodge, dyeing and colouring their heads to make them look younger. There was clipping them out, disguising their legs, manes and tails to sell them back maybe to people who once had owned them."*

The Townsleys did a lot of dealing with the local Co-operative Society as well as other large businesses. *"We sold them carts, harness and horses, and got them back in part exchange when they wanted something different. We had different HALF WIDE FLATS in the area who worked for firms among the horses. They kept tabs on things and informed the Families when they wanted an exchange or a deal."*

The Townsley's travelled far and wide in search of good horses, many of which were bought as unbroken, for this meant they could be obtained at very low prices. Breaking in a horse was demanding on both man and animal; the Townsleys had their own methods. *"They used to put them in chains pulling heavy loads through the fields and up the moors. They rubbed their legs with a sort of liniment and shod them with specially weighted shoes to make them lift their feet up into a high action. There was a special long shafted breaking cart that was also used. If a horse got above itself, it would be driven by three or more drivers in a day. Yes they broke horses hearts when they got above themselves."*

Other methods that were meted out in the close confines of a stable yard may sound extreme to those who have never been involved with requiring instant obedience from an animal. *"Yes, we could always master dodgy greys. The boys could put them through it with their Muller and London whips. I have seen horses thrashed, and really thrashed when the boys set about them. I have seen them trying to get up the walls in the yard; and you could see them trembling when they met their masters."*

Tales of a Lakeland Gypsy

There was no place for sentimentality when breaking a new horse. It was understood that the animal was subservient to its owner. The horse was the means by which members of the Family were able to earn a living. The animal had to be mastered, and it had to obey the rules. Once it had absorbed that message, the horses that worked for the Townsleys were treated to the best of care and attention. *"The horses that we used every day had to be fed every morning before we got our breakfasts. That was one of my jobs as soon as I was old enough."*

John's father and his Uncle, Big Charlie, had a reputation for standing no nonsense from a horse, they had the ability to break them in within a very short time. An old timer told John Townsley that he had seen his dad working with unbroken horses. *"I have seen MAGREMS [horses], crazy wild head cases that needed sorting out, new ones from Ireland, going up the walls of the yards. Within a day or two he had sickened them, and then they were like lambs."* John Townsley junior recalled that his father had only failed to break one horse. *"There was just one horse that beat my dad, and he shot it. He cut the body up into bits and dropped them down John Pit near Lowca."*

John Pit was a former coal mine, where a disused and deep shaft was the recipient of many unwanted objects. *"The knacker business was not really operating in those days, and the money paid for knacker's meat was not worth picking up."*

"When my dad got the new horses home, they were turned into the fields, and people would come and pick out the one they wanted to buy. A lot would go through the rings and auction mart at Cockermouth, and also sold behind the auction on Fairfield."

Some of the best horses that the Family had were Welsh cobs. They had a good reputation for speed and stamina and were ideal to work the rough roads along which the Family travelled. *"When it was getting to the end of a calling district, and they turned their heads for home, that's when they used to hit top speed. The Welsh cobs were noted for their good legs and bone. They could stand up to the rough roads on which they were driven and they did many miles in a day. They were looked after, and had the best of everything because these were the horses that made the money, and were sought after by delivery men. They were fit muscled up machines. There was Irish horses, and Caldbeck bred fell ponies, but for a road horse, day in and day out, you could not beat a Welsh Cob or an Arab Welsh Cob cross."*

The best of the horses that were broken in were always kept by the Family and put to work between the shafts of the fish or pot carts. There was an ongoing need to replace horses that were working every day, with young and stronger animals that were fit enough for the long runs into the high country. The type of work they did, and the rounds they covered were rotated to get the maximum work out of the animals.

Members of the Family were also skilled at treating horse ailments, when they often used old fashioned remedies that had been passed down through generations. *"In the old days, there was a few veterinaries, but the Elders used to doctor the horses themselves. They used to do things like bleeding, taking away blood in large amounts, sometimes a bucketful, and blistering horses. All kinds of herbs were used in making liniments and tonics. They used things out of the fields, which cost nothing, to get heat out of joints and feet. When they were fiery, they had a special recipe to give them to cool them down. They made special liquids for treating sores."* John explained that young two year old horses that were being broken had very soft skin that could rub and chafe when the horse was put in harness. *"We used to bathe the horses with warm water and alum. Until their skin hardened, their shoulders were very soft and tender."*

In some country areas, where veterinaries were few and far between, qualified medical treatment for the horses of country folk was not easy to obtain. Often, as John explained, *"In the old days, farmers, carters and delivery men would turn to the travellers for a cure. No doubt, some of the boys would make it out to be more serious than it was to enable him to trade it for another."*

On more than one occasion, the Townsleys bought in a good horse that had gone lame, at an extremely low price. Using expertise and knowledge that was built up over many years of practical experience, that same horse was back into work within a very short time. All that was needed was a week of treatment and rest. *"There was some old people, travellers who lived in Workington who had a favourite horse. It had gone lame on and off for a while so they asked my dad to look at it. He bought this horse off them, and in a short time it was back in harness. It had a few problems, but my dad cured them all."*

John's brother in law, William Lowther who was a fine horseman, also had a reputation for being able to treat horses' ailments. *"He doctored his own horses, and also attended to country peoples' lame and sick horses with his own remedies that had been handed down through generations of his own, and his wife's families."*

There were plenty of old and lame horses about, for many people, while they could not afford the price of a top class working animal, could manage to pay the lower prices asked for animals that had seen better days. In much the same way as policemen nowadays cast an eye over motor vehicles for a lack of a tax disc, damaged bodywork, or worn tyres, in the days when the horse actually provided the horse power, the MUSKERS [police] were on the look out for any animals that were not fit for the job in hand.

"MUSKERS or OWNIES were always eyeing, and weighing up old TITS [horses], and walking round yokes, vetting them. They used to look for GALLOWAYS [working horses] that had scalded shoulders, and owt that had a bit IF, about it. They were also on the look-out for people ill treating horses. A lot of old greys were dodgy in those days, because a lot of FLATTY ANTLE couldn't afford to pay for a real good roadster. There was no knackers trade as such in those days, anything was used to pull a cart."

The Townsleys themselves were not unknown for handing out harsh treatment to a horse that was trying to get the better of them. When John Townsley junior met up with a group of travelling Gypsies who were camped on Kirkland Green, during the time he was working the high country in the 1930's, they told him about a meeting with his great grandfather and grandmother in the Lamplugh area. The Elders stopped for a yarn about the old times, and the deals that were done. Old Townsley told the Gypsy, *"We are just making our way home, and this horse we are driving has worked me all day. I couldn't set about it in among people and houses, but I am just going to let him see who is the boss."*

The old Gypsy followed the Townsleys for part of the way because they were on their way to visit other Gypsy families who had camped on the Cloffocks, a traditional camping ground in the Workington area. *"He drew his whip, and I have never seen a man give a horse a MILLEN like it. One minute they were on the road, the next over the dyke and into the fields. The next salute they were back on the hard roads and had gone over Dean Moor common, out of sight and going for home."*

On occasions, if a horse was not found to be suitable for working the Townsley way, it would be sold on to another owner. John Townsley senior set out one day for Cockermouth market. The horse he drove was described by his son as *"a pig of a horse. It didn't want to go backwards or forwards, but it was a beauty to look at."* The cart was loaded with scrap metal, plumber's lead, and a quantity of brass, that made a significant weight for the horse to pull over the ten miles of distance between Harrington and Cockermouth. When John Townsley senior arrived at Cockermouth, a crowd of dealers were congregated in Huntsman's Yard, weighing up the form of horses, or where there was a likely touch to be made. They eyed up John Townsley's horse as he drove into the yard. The fine looking animal, pulling a heavy load, caught the eye of a dealer. He stepped forward.

"Are you looking for trade with your horse? I have a fine driving horse to suit you, John."

"He will have to be a good 'un to beat my horse" replied the elder Townsley, making no mention of the incalcitrant qualities of his good looking horse, but he went into the stables to look over the horses that the dealer had on offer. *"Pull this one out and let me see it go."*

Duly satisfied, a deal was struck, and the horses were exchanged with John Townsley pocketing a few pounds extra for his "good looking" horse. His acquisition proved to be a real winner of a deal, for once in the cart, the new Townsley horse went "up hill and down dale" without any bother. Two days later however, the other dealer had come to realise his mistake; he sent a telegram to the Townsley's to come and collect *"the good looker, we can do nowt with it"*. The horse had run amok in the yard and kicked a cart to pieces. When John senior went to collect the "good looker", he let the dealer know that he had bought the horse as it stood in the shafts, " as seen", and never asked any questions about its character. A Townsley deal had worked again. No money was exchanged or returned, the Townsleys were better off by an additional horse.

This sort of dealing was commonplace, people were always on the look-out for something that looked more impressive than their neighbour owned. *"People with horses then were like people with cars today. It was who had the best driving horse in traps, gigs or flat carts. farmers, milkmen, and delivery people were always looking for the best, and my elders were just waiting to oblige them."*

When the Family was horse dealing they were always willing to demonstrate what a horse could do. Any animal in which a potential buyer was interested was yoked up, put through its paces, examined and handled before a deal was struck. *"Nine times out of ten, we wanted money on the side as well, and the countryman had often dealed away a much better horse, on many an occasion."*

The Townsley horses were always fed on the best of food. Even when they were out working on the road, a bag of oats and some hay was slung under the cart so that the horse could be fed during the day. There were plenty of water troughs tucked into hedgerows where the horse could get a drink of fresh flowing water. *"We used to get crushed oats from West's saw mill and corn mill at Branthwaite".* This was sufficient to see the horses through a day of hard work until it was time for their heads to be turned for home. *"They would fly down those hills like birds on the wing. They knew they were making for a warm stable with a good trough full of oats, a manger full of hay and a good clean straw bed. They were fed like fighting cocks on the best food. We also mixed extra vitamins in with their oats and stamina proven and minerals."*

The Family were also involved in horse dealing with the many travelling circuses that paid visits to the county. A regular spot on which they used to pitch their tents, was on the Cloffocks, situated on the outskirts of the town of Workington. This was also a traditional stopping over place for travelling Gypsies. *"My grandfather and dad used to supply all the circuses that came into the area, they would let us know what they were looking for; what colour they wanted."* The circus horses were taken in part exchange and were described by John as rejects, as far as the circus was concerned, but they were sold on for other jobs, such as pulling carts of rags or scrap. A sentimentalist would say this was a sad demise from the glitzy trappings of the circus ring with its smell of sawdust, and lights; the horse probably could tell no great difference, and just accepted its lot.

One regular request that the Townsleys used to get was for a team of matched black horses to pull funeral hearses for the many undertakers in the district. The animals were resplendent in gleaming black harness, with stately black plumes waving above their heads, as immaculately groomed, they added a solemn dignity to a funeral procession.

With such large numbers of horses on the roads, the village smithy used to be a busy place, not only for the practical tasks of ensuring that horses were shod, but as a centre of communication. It was regarded as an important meeting place to gather scraps of gossip, while the smith was hammering out the shoes from his bars of iron, and fitting them to the horse. The local "crack" was accompanied by the hiss of cooling iron, and the acrid smell of smouldering hoof. John could recall two black-smith's shops in Workington, one that belonged to Jim Farish and his son, was in Washington Street in the heart of the town, while the other, where Ernie Huddart was the smith, was on the road out of the town to Whitehaven. *"Farmers and others used to leave messages regarding business deals they wanted done."*

John's favourite smithy was one out in the high country. *"I used to like calling to get a horse shod at Josey Edmondson's Beck Smithy at Lamplugh. He used to talk about all the local folk lore and things that had happened in the past, and the present. He was a gamecock breeder. Locals and others just used to call in the smithy for the crack"*. The Townsleys used to collect more than "crack", for they also bought the scrap metal that was of no further use to the smith, but would earn them a few shillings in the scrap side of their business.

The Townsley girls were a good advertisement for the docility of their horses. Farmers, and their wives needed the use of a horse and trap to take goods to market, or generally get about the countryside. *"This was the only transport. Some liked high stepping horses, others likes a faster, low action for speed. Some had market and spring carts for carrying produce to sell on the market stalls, and others liked tub traps which were safe for the children. They were sometimes called governess carts. Others liked the showy traps and lightweight gigs for faster roading."* The country folk used to see the Townsley girls skilful handling of the driving horses and appreciate the sound and trustworthy nature of the animals. Often, when the girls went about their rounds, they had a spare horse tied to the back of the cart. It was not unknown for the very horse that was taking one of the Family into the high country to be sold to a farmer's wife, and the return journey home made with the spare horse pulling the cart. *"Some of the farmers had to have a really reliable horse, for some of them would get into the public house after they had finished their business in the auction mart. They would get so drunk, the horse had to take them home."*

There was also a market for mules, donkeys and ponies that were sold for working in the mines or quarries. The small animals were used to pull the laden tubs of coal from the workings to the shafts. They spent all their lives underground, frequently in complete darkness, where they inhaled the dust of the stifling conditions for every day of their lives. They shared this adversity along with their handlers for men were employed specially to care for the pit ponies, and as so often happens, they became very attached to their charges. When the annual holiday came round, the ponies were taken to the surface to enjoy clean fresh air for a brief part of their lives. *"The pit ponies maybe used to get up out of the pits for a week in the summer, to graze on the nearby pit fields. They used to draw off from the herd those that were worn out, and finished for work down the mines. That's when we always had some ready on hand, just waiting for the mine managers to come and have a look, and buy what he wanted."* There was also an old superstition that it was lucky to run a donkey with a herd of cattle, so many an animal was supplied for that purpose.

There were other dealers as wide awake as the Townsleys who were always ready to unload poor horses on an unsuspecting purchaser. *"You had to be wary of all the various dodges, SHAN GRAFTERS, runaways and all the physical complaints. Some people bought dodgy horses because they were a lot cheaper and all they could afford, but they caused a lot of trouble and upsets; they were misfits."*

Other tricks were tried when the Townsleys went to Ireland to buy horses, for although the country had a fine reputation for the quality of the horses that were bred there, the sellers were up to their tricks. *"The Elders used to talk about all the tricks the Irish men would try on when selling. Some men would dress themselves up in Catholic priests clothing, and they talked in short religious phrases. They tried to sell horses with false papers regarding the breeding and the blood lines. Others would say that the*

Tales of a Lakeland Gypsy

horses had already been in harness in commercial carts, but the truth was they were as green as grass; they were right off the Bog. Some Irishmen would say the horses had been bred and reared on the Church lands and the proceeds of the sales went to the Church. Then there were others who dressed up as country gentleman, and pretended that one of their mates worked for them who would demonstrate the worthiness of a horse. They were known to dope wild, or runaway MAGREMS. It was a trick to make them seem docile. It took the fire out of them, and kept them quiet for a few days."

When the Townsleys made these trips to Ireland, they went as a team, so they were able to look after each others interests. When there was a large number of horses to be handled, it needed sharp eyes to ensure that none that they had been bought were stolen back before they reached the boat to bring them back to England. Even then, there were still opportunities for horses to be stolen on the drive back to Cumbria. Guards had to be mounted on overnight stops to ensure that there were the same number of animals to continue the journey the following day. *"In the old days, they used to say that coming over Beattock was bad for the horse thieves, and also for the bad weather."*

With the introduction of mechanisation on farms, and the development of the car and bus for transport services, there was less demand for horses as working animals. John gave up dealing in horses, after his family split up through marriage and the onset of the second world war. *"In the 37's and 38's I used to buy some good driving cobs that I used to sell to local farmers, and local users for commercial deliveries."* Working on the premise that if you can't beat them, join them, John turned to mechanisation to carry on his trading business. *"In late 1938, I sold the horses we were using and bought two motor vans; one for my sister, and one for me. But come early 1940, fish was hard to get, and we were also rationed for petrol."* The army claimed John, and wedlock claimed his sister. Part of John Townsley's life that he had loved, working with horses, was effectively over.

Loading the hay, Loweswater 1913

Horse Sale, Wigton, 1994

Chapter Nine

HORSE CHARACTERS

Of all the horses with which John Townsley's family had dealings, it was inevitable that some emerged as being rather different from all the others. The walls of rooms in the Townsley homes down Potters' Lonnin' in Harrington, were hung with drawings and pictures of horses that had been special to the family over the years. Even today, John Townsley claims that he would rather drive a good road horse, "that has everything in it", than the finest Rolls Royce.

What does John look for in a good road horse?

"If it has a special colour, height confirmation, good bone all put together as a good 'un should be. It should also have a terrific action, and a temperament that enables it to be driven by a child even in heavy traffic on the busy road. If it is a registered stallion, and has passed the strictest veterinary and government tests, then you have got a real 'un. If it be a mare, with all the same credentials, then you have a rare commodity, a precious asset."

John has had a few of this type through his hands during the years when he was working and dealing with horses. From an early age, he knew what to look for; he gained his experience in learning about horses from his Elders and by following the Family ways. The accumulation of knowledge was handed down from generation to generation.

In their every day jobs around the towns and countryside of Cumberland and the north east of England, there was always some member of the Family on the look out for a good horse. Some were brought to their notice by a proud owner boasting at a country market, or in his local pub about what his horse could do. Tips were passed on to the Family, with the informant receiving a few pounds on the side. This was invariably followed by some shrewd and seemingly irresistible dealings that brought the good horses into the Family's hands.

"An old GADGE came up to Grandfather John Townsley and said, I saw a good horse yesterday John, and it was flying."

"Flying?" queried the elder Townsley, *"I never saw yan pen feathered, nivver mind full flighted."*

Other horses that were brought to the attention of the family were those beyond the control of their owner, who was often only too pleased to be rid of an animal that thrashed about its stable, almost clambering up the walls due to a surfeit of energy. These horses were taken in part exchange by the Family, and the relieved former owner was only too happy to take one of inferior quality, but which was much easier to handle. Once a difficult horse had been subjected to the Family treatment, it was only a matter of a few days before it became manageable, and turned out to be what

92

Tales of a Lakeland Gypsy

John Townsley described as " a winner." The Family even took some horses as a part settlement of debts, for any moneys owed to the Family had to be settled in either cash or kind.

All these special equine characters that passed through their hands, are woven into the folk lore of John Townsley's family history. One of the most highly rated was GUIDING STAR, the horse, which in John Townsley's opinion, was one of the finest that they ever owned.

This is the tale of Guiding Star, *"the horse that ruled the night"*. In 1889, Grandfather John Townsley was at Rosley Fair with his two sons, Big Charlie and John. Rosley was one of the oldest fairs in the north for dealing in sheep, horses and cattle. It was held, once a month, just a few miles outside the north Cumbrian town of Wigton. The Townsleys attended the Fair on a regular basis, and on one particular occasion, when they had sold all the horses they had taken with them, they looked round for others that they could buy to *"knock into shape"*. A young animal tethered to the back of a road caravan caught their eye. The Townsleys approached the owner, who was sitting on the steps of his caravan.

They asked him his price, but were told to *"Forget about it"*. He added that several people, who had also been attracted by the quality of the horse, had bought it from him, but all found they could do nothing with it; and it had always been returned to him. The Townsleys persisted, there was something about the horse that caught their eye. Eventually a sale was agreed, and they bought the horse at their price.

"They yoked their own horse into the flat cart and tied the new horse to the end board. They had twenty five miles to go and it was getting dark. It was after midnight when they got on top of Winscales Moor. The old man said, ' Pull up lads and we will yoke this new gray up. We'll put him between the shafts and see how he shapes.' At first, they couldn't do anything with him, until the old man said,' Set about him lads with those whips.'

So the lads set about this GALLOWAY with their MULLER whips. The old man kept egging them on with shouts of, 'Lay on, I think he's a coward.' By then, this horse was knocked nearly out of shape, and they had mastered it. They drove it home, and it proved to be an all time great."

They named the horse Guiding Star. *"They used to come from all over the country just to see this horse in harness; this horse was a machine driven by Townsleys only."*

The Townsley brothers, always ready for a bet, threw out challenges to anybody who had a horse that they thought could match Guider over short and long distances. But nothing could touch it and they always won.

Big Charlie and his brother John were in partnership in the horse dealing side of the business, and on one occasion, they returned from delivering horses in the Egremont area to find a message urging them to drive to Scotland to see a dying relative. *"Leave Guiding Star in the spindle gig, and give him a good feed. We will be leaving when we have had something to eat."* They drove on, none stop, through the night, and reached Glasgow the next day. That was a distance of 120 miles. They stayed long enough for

93

the relative's funeral, and then drove back to High Harrington with Guiding Star in the shafts.

"This was a feat never known of, and never to be equalled. Travellers and country Mush made up poetry about this horse. They headed one piece, Guiding Star, the Road Machine that rules the Night."

That horse was kept in the Townsley family until it died. *"The girls used to hawk with him; they used to go with metals to Newcastle, and do a bit of trading on the way there, and on the way back."* This involved a round journey of about 180 miles

The family had another road horse at about the same time as they owned Guiding Star: this was a mare called MARY SWAN. *"They said after driving her mile after mile, on long journeys, you darn't drop the WANG on her coming back home, or she would kick the cart to bits."*

The Brothers had another notable horse at around the same time. This was called "NIGGER". John Townsley described it as a 16 hands black driving machine. *"It was used for fast roading in the fish and herring carts. It used to be washed, and polished with a silk cloth on a Sunday until its coat gleamed"*, but although there were many horses offered for sale, Nigger was not among them.

John Townsley's brother was known as Young Charlie to distinguish him from his uncle, Big Charlie. He was usually called Chuck. One of his favourite horses was a Welsh cob chestnut mare called DOLLY. He used to drive her into the High Country and beyond, every day. *"Every day was a spit out for these muscled up road machines that were bred for the open road. Distance meant nothing to them. All my sisters used to drive these roadsters, buying and selling anything that was profitable."*

The Townsley girls knew how to handle Dolly, *"They knew her ways and her soft spots"*. Unlike Guiding Star and Nigger, Dolly was available for sale. One traveller who always camped on the Cloffocks came to buy her but the Family tried to put him off. He had seen the lasses hawking about with her and was under the impression that if they could handle Dolly, so could he. He walked her down to Workington from our yard, and next day tried to yoke her. The horse proved to be uncooperative, it jerked away from its strange and rough handler. Unknown to this traveller, a police inspector was standing on a road that overlooked the camping ground. He watched the struggle between man and mare before he eventually decided to intervene. He walked down the steps and onto the Cloffocks to stop the rough treatment that was being given to the horse. He is reputed to have said to the traveller, *"If you don't stop abusing that mare, I will lock you up in a cell. I have watched you; I know that mare, you had better take it back to High Harrington."*

Dolly was walked back and exchanged for another horse that was easier for the traveller to handle. *"The following day, she was yoked up and out hawking with the lasses."*

Another favourite horse of the family around the time of the first world war, was one that was called "THREE CORNERED JIM". He was another fast road horse. *"He had a running YUK, and a BOK SPAVIN, but he could trot."*

Tales of a Lakeland Gypsy

Jim was admired by many horse people. *"Although my dad and his brother Big Charlie were partners in the horse dealing, Jim was our horse. All kinds of people wanted to buy him. We sold him once or twice, but my dad knew he would always get him back."* After Jim had been returned from yet another owner who could not handle him, John's dad decided to keep him, for he was a particular favourite horse, especially of the girls. *"It will be a long time before I sell him again,"* John Townsley senior vowed.

Mother Ellen agreed for she also realised the working potential and reliability of the big horse. But her husband's intentions if well meant, were short lived, as John Townsley recalled what happened. *"My father, and uncle Big Charlie had to go to Egremont to deliver three horses that they had sold. Jim was yoked up in the trap, and the others were tied behind. My mother Ellen, who stood nearly six feet tall and was built like an athlete, waited all day for them coming back. She was up and down the lane waiting for the two men, but it was not until the evening she could hear them coming."*

At the sound of the hooves, Mother Ellen immediately realised there was something wrong, for the clopping sounds that carried down the lane, indicated that it was not Jim between the shafts of the trap, but another horse. *"They pulled up in the lonnin' and my mother went mad. She said, where's Jim?"*

"We have had a real good deal for these three horses", was the reply, as the two men indicated the three animals tied behind the trap. *"She threw her coat off and set up to Big Charlie. She shouted, ' I knew there was something on this morning.' She carried on for some time, but in the end calmed down because they had done very well in the deal."* Some months later they got Jim back in an exchange deal, but he was later sold to a Carlisle man.

"One day, this man was travelling over Eden Bridge, trying to outshine a country gentleman with his flash turnout. The country MUSH said, Will you get out of my way with that old horse?

The Gypsy man challenged the MUSH to a race over ten miles. He beat the country GADGE out of sight to pick up the wager."

Shortly after the first world war some people from the Maryport area, that John described as "elderly", went across to Ireland to buy two or three horses for use in their fruit hawking business. *"There was one horse in particular which cost a higher price than normal. My dad was told by various people that this mare was something special, so he made it his business to have a look at it. My dad liked what he saw, and challenged the two brothers to have a deal. The two old men used to like a bit of horse trading, so one Sunday, they came over with this horse in their gig."*

They were entertained to the usual hospitality that Mother Ellen provided for visitors, and were shown all the horses in the stables. Different animals were pulled out, they were harnessed and put through their paces; some were trotted in hand to show off their action. Eventually, a horse was selected that was suited to their needs, and a deal was struck. *"They put their new horse in their gig and set off home, highly delighted with their new Welsh cob, which they kept for many years."*

Tales of a Lakeland Gypsy

That same night, the Townsley's new acquisition was yoked into a trap and tried out. *"They gave her the name Molly Malloy. People used to come and watch her trot in harness. She had a low cut action, and was a flyer; any man would have been proud to own her."* Molly was a favourite of John's sister who drove her every day in the High Country, but this was another horse that the Townsleys sold on a number of occasions.

This was part of the Townsley dealing strategy, for they were only too aware that these road horses thrived on long distance work, and were always likely to be returned to them when found unsuitable for short distance work. *"She wanted to do distance work, not amble round delivering milk. She was in her element when you let her go down the road to do her thing; and that was to trot."*

One of the Townsleys' best horses was bought by Mother Ellen and came as a result of a tip off from a farmer friend who passed on the information that another farmer had just acquired two good galloways. *"My mother said she would go right away; she knew the farmer liked a deal".* After the usual offerings of country hospitality, and some hours of haggling, Mother Ellen finally succeeded in buying them at a price to her liking, *"She chucked it for 14 quid".* The new horses were tied to the tail board of Mother Ellen's cart, and they trotted behind as she drove back to the yard. *"She put them in the stable awaiting the boys, and my dad and Big Charlie. She didn't know that she had bought one of the best driving horses in Mother England."*

They soon realised this after yoking one of them, a chestnut mare, and giving her a day or two of distance driving. *"They knew they had some horse, they called her MAGGIE MURPHY, THE CHESTNUT FLYER."* John's sister Lizzie drove Maggie Murphy most days, it was one of her favourite horses. Together, they would cover thirty to forty miles as they delivered fish and traded in the High Country.

Maggie Murphy was involved with the Family for many years, for although they parted with her on a number of occasions, *"letting her go in deals to FLATS, it was always on the understanding that we could buy her back."* John told of one such deal. *"There was a travelling man camped on the Cloffocks at Workington, he had just come back from the Isle of Man. he had been trucking and trading with the Family, but he was running out of ROWDY. He had just been coming up to our stables too many times, and he was losing his money. He was just out of his depth. He comes one Sunday morning into the lane, and had dinner with us. He said he was leaving with his family for Carlisle, but he had nothing to pull his horse drawn wagon. Being a good friend of my dad's, he buys Maggie Murphy, the legend horse. The Boys and Dealers had never seen anything like her in Carlisle, she was all the travellers could talk about. They used to drive her out of Carlisle and over the Border for a day's dealing, and the Boys would be outside the PEEVERS [pubs] in Caldewgate waiting for her being driven home loaded with BAGS. They said she used to make sparks fly taking Caldewgate by storm."*

Another horse that Lizzie Townsley used to like to drive was Bob, a chestnut bought from a dealer in Egremont. *"Roading mile after mile in the depths of winter was play lakin' for him. Country people marvelled at the way Lizzie drove. After her last hawking call in the depths of winter, with up to 18 miles to drive home, the farmers used to light her lamps, put on a bag of potatoes, and leps of hay."* While Lizzie was enjoying a hot cup of tea to warm her for the journey home, a lad would hold Bob's head until Lizzie clambered aboard the turnout, finding a soft seat on the hay. Then it was off for home. *"They used to say that when Lizzie was on her way back home and got to the top of Dean Moor, she used to ask Bob to go, and it was like a bird on the wing. He was a real flyer."*

On one occasion, Lizzie was driving Bob home along a clear road, with no traffic to cause any hindrance. She gave Bob his head and let him go. Lizzie was a great driver of horses, and whenever she was returning home, she always made a point of trying to beat her own record for getting there. *"She revelled in the challenge of being born around horses. One night when she was coming back home she was driving Bob so fast, that both the axle and the wheels dropped off the cart. It was half a mile further on before she managed to pull Bob up. She was sitting on the body of the cart that Bob had just dragged along the road."*

Neither horse nor rider were any worse for that experience but there was the problem of a damaged cart to take care of. It didn't bother Lizzie; she managed to get the cart to a nearby farm to ensure that everything that was in it, was taken care of. She was able to leave it, secure in the knowledge that some of "the boys" would return to collect it the following day. All that was left for Lizzie to do was complete her journey home. This she did by riding home to Harrington riding bareback on Bob.

Ready to work.

John Townsley bids goodbye to Civvie Street.

Chapter Ten

FOR KING, COUNTRY, AND SELF

The latter years of the 1930's brought tremendous changes to Ellen Townsley's family. As John was the only surviving son, much of the responsibility for running the family business fell on his shoulders. Most of his sisters had married and as was the custom in Gypsy families, had taken with them a dowry, which consisted of a sum of money proportionate to their share of the business. In 1939, when war broke out, there was only John and one sister who still lived with Mother Ellen, to carry on dealing and trading.

"We had vans by that time, but when war started we had difficulty getting the petrol. We still carried on trading, but didn't go into the high country like we did in the old days. We carried on dealing and selling from a horse and cart in different parts of Workington, but we could see it was only a matter of time before I had to go in the army."

Eventually, John's sister married and sure enough, he received his call up papers to join the army. He sold his share of the fish business to some cousins, finalised his own personal family arrangements, and then travelled by train to the south of England, where he reported to a training camp near Andover.

"There I got a shock. The food was poor, the training was hard, and the regime was very military. It was a case of you are here, and you are going to be put through the rigours of a varied form of training."

At the end of the week he received his first army pay packet, which also came as a shock. *"You marched up to the officer's table and gave him a salute; you picked up your pay packet, then saluted again and smartly marched away. All for ten shillings. What was I going to do with that sort of money?"* Supper in the NAAFI, stamps for writing home, cigarettes, polish for boots and badges, all had to come out of the regulation ten shillings a week. *"That was no good to me."*

Like all the other raw recruits who were called up for war time service, John was given three months basic training. The trainees were then forwarded to other training courses in more specialised skills. John was sent to Newark on a mechanical training course, which included driving caterpillar tractors. This was much more to his liking than the regimentation of drill and endless cleaning of brass and webbing. It also led to the opportunity that gave John his first glimpse into what other possibilities army life could offer.

"I was sent down to Newport Pagnell where things were a lot easier. I was in a pub one night and could see there was a lot of dodgy business going on." Among the tightly clustered crowd of civilians and uniformed men, he realised that there were deals being made. He explained that after a life time spent in the business, one became very

aware of the signs to look for. He watched, he waited and took note of everything that was going on. When he visited the pub again, he struck up a conversation with a local man; he asked him the score. He was told, *"If you have anything like black market stuff or CHOREY, there are men who come in here to buy."*

So that set John thinking of how he could turn army life to his own advantage. *"I knew there were thousands of people in the country dodging their call up, so that changed my outlook. I said to myself, I am here to do whatever I am asked to do, but I am going to have part of the action for myself."*

He took the opportunity to do a little dealing on the side, but that was small stuff compared to the big break that came his way when he was posted to Hull. The busy east coast port was a turmoil of boats, that were coming and going in such numbers that the normal dock labour force was unable to physically handle all the unloading of cargo from merchant ships bringing much needed supplies. Soldiers were drafted in to help them, and John found himself working alongside civilian dockers, welders, crane drivers, longshoremen, and lorry drivers that made up the anonymous, yet essential cogs in the machine that kept essential supplies flowing into the country. Although he continued to wear his army khaki, and had the identity of a soldier, John was absorbed into the teeming workforce that was free of the regimentation of military life.

He was billeted in a private house, which was far more comfortable than an army barracks, for the elderly people with whom he stayed made him so welcome and comfortable that it seem like home from home. Each morning he went to work at the docks where his particular job was to drive the high cranes *"that were perched up on top of the buildings."*

The soldiers were given a daily cash allowance to buy their meals at one of the many large canteens on the dock sides, but John found there was rarely any need to use his money. When the time for a break came, he asked a member of the crew of the ship that he was unloading if there was any SCRAN for him. *"Certainly soldier"* he was told, *"Come aboard."* There he was treated to the hospitality of the ship's crew. Hot meals, drinks, cigarettes were all available to him., and of a much better quality than was obtainable in the dock side canteens.

"Then they would give me cartons of cigarettes that I sold to the dockers and welders who were working on the dock side. They also gave me nylons and I was able to make good money selling these."

Some of the merchant seamen and dockers, who were also keen to take advantage of the potential money making opportunities of the Black Market, were apprehensive about taking such goods off the docks, for security was much tighter for them than it was for the men in uniform. Police boxes were manned round the clock, security was tight, and there were checks of body and pack, before the workforce could pass through the dock gates. John had no such worries and often carried goods out for other men without fear of being stopped. *"The police never stopped me, because I was a soldier and could move freely about. Some of the police were also taking black market goods off the docks."*

Tales of a Lakeland Gypsy

John went to work every day carrying his big army pack which he had squared up on the inside with cardboard. That made it easier to pack with cartons of cigarettes. *"I had my overalls sticking out of the top so that things didn't look too suspicious. I could carry goods like this twice a day, at dinner time and at night. No one in the army bothered, there was no one in charge of us, we just were able to come and go as we pleased."*

At night in the Paragon Hotel, John met up with the men for whom he had been carrying the black market goods away from the docks, and he was always well paid for his trouble. *"It was nearly always womens' wear that they wanted me to carry off. There were plenty of customers for it. Leading lights of the town were good customers, they were buying for their wives and girl friends. Even upper class women were prepared to buy it, sometimes with their bodies, even though their husbands were away in the war. The black market was rife, there was always plenty of money to change hands when you knew where to look for it."*

He recalled that the people of Hull were very hospitable towards the soldiers. *"The men working on the docks were well paid, but we just had our 10/- a week. I used to go to a club and people would buy me drinks and food, they were very sociable."*

When the opportunity came to take a weekend's leave, John travelled home to West Cumberland to visit his mother who had moved in to live with one of her married daughters. *"I borrowed a suitcase and filled it with nylons. I had my big pack and that was full of American cigarettes, Camel, Philip Morris and various other brands. I had been given all these by the foreign merchant navy crews of the boats I was working on. When I got home, I soon realised there was no problem there ; a ready black market was already operating."*

The easy pickings of Hull came to an end when John was transferred to a camp near Helensburgh in Scotland and although he was sent to work at the docks once again, this time he was involved in loading cargo on to ships that were bound for the middle east. He had lost the comforts and home cooking of his Hull billet, and also the rewards that the black market brought his way. In the Scottish camp, *"the food was rubbish and the tea, you could never drink. All this for ten shillings a week."* It wasn't long however before he discovered that even there, living in inhospitable Scotland, there were ways that could be found to supplement an army pay packet.

Whisky was included among the cargo that had to be loaded aboard the transport ships. Here indeed was an opportunity to make something on the side. *"The Boys used to knock off spirits when they were on the night shift and hide it under the wooden floor boards of the barrack huts. The railway line was nearby, and a train used to run right into Glasgow from Helensburgh. On a Saturday morning, the Boys would go out of camp by a back way, cross the fields and take the Whisky train to Glasgow to sell the LOOT they had saved all week."*

That posting did not last long enough to be of any great benefit to John, but his next move to Cairnryan, was even worse. There, the only commodity that was available for sale was fish. *"In our spare time we used to fish, and catch all sorts, plaice, mackerel and cod,"* and although John was a master of the fish hawking trade, it was unfortunate for him that there was no one that wanted to buy it. Even unloading the boats that came from Ireland brought no perks that he could turn to his advantage, and he described the area as a *"dump with nowhere to go, and nothing to do. They didn't even have a place where you could get a cup of tea."*

He asked for and was given a move, but a series of different postings brought little opportunity to work for himself, until he was sent to Aldershot where he teamed up with an ex - costermonger from London. *"We weighed up the run of things and realised there was business to be done in the black market in a local town."* The camp and its surrounding areas had all sorts of tradesmen, and a lot of Irishmen were employed on government contract work. There was a a readily available market waiting to be tapped. *"We bought and traded with everybody; it was a good place. There was stacks of money about in the pubs. The beer used to flow at the weekends when you got to know the local characters. There was stacks of women about in the pubs, and they wanted to know you for whatever."*

Once their army day's work was done, Johm and his partner also made extra money for themselves by working on a caravan site at nights. *"The money was OK and we got good food and anything else that was on offer".* Many of those with whom John was trading were quite happy for the war to continue, for the black market was providing them with a good living. *"When socialising with them, they would say, it's only those that have no one to shield them, or pull strings for them that are called up to the forces. If you know the right people, you can get fixed up with an occupational job that makes you exempt."*

That posting lasted a number of months and gave John sufficient time to get to know all the locals, to discover the draft dodgers, and realise that fiddling was rife. *"I would say it was a free for all; I did whatever job I had to do in the Forces, but number one priority was to look after myself, and be on the look out all the time. We were into FENCING, whatever came up."*

Britain in wartime was a country that experienced shortages in almost every commodity, and there was always a buyer for goods that became available even by dubious means. John was stationed in a camp that had all sorts of things that were unavailable to the civilian population, especially foodstuffs. *"Even the officers were into CHORING, especially for their MOTES."*

He explained that at night, the woods surrounding the camp came alive. *"Tackle was planted in the undergrowth everywhere, to be picked up. SKIDS was wanted by everybody, TUGGERY was in demand. Business people were desperate for goods, and we almost had a free hand to supply them. We used to KIP with CUSHTY BARRIE MOTES all night; some were officers MOTES. They were real clients."*

All this dealing was taking place among the normal regulated procedings of army life, where most of the other soldiers were totally unaware of what was happening, *"and maybe just as well"* was John's reflected comment. But in spite of looking after his own interests, and as evidence of the satisfactory way in which he carried out his soldier's role, John was offered promotion to NCO rank. He declined to take it, even though a small increase of pay accompanied a higher rank. He was concerned that the extra burden of responsibility that promotion entailed might have restricted his own activities.

The good life, however, came to an end with a spell of embarkation leave, which he spent at home in Cumberland, before an overseas posting to the Far East. *"We went round South Africa in a convoy of other troopships and we were escorted by ships of the Royal Navy, that covered us on both the port and starboard sides. We were at sea for weeks, and it was rough. We just KIPPED anywhere we could."*

Journey's end was Bombay, where after embarkation there was only a brief respite before John and his unit were transferred for an Indian train journey to Calcutta which lasted for five days, and five nights. The heat and discomfort of the long journey was only relieved when they made a short stay at Alipore Camp. *"There was a race track there and I used to go on a Saturday afternoon. I was lucky and backed a few winners."*

After a brief stay in the transit camp, John was moved into what he described as *"the wilds of North Bengal. It was wild desolate country, but very hot, twenty four hours a day"*. From there, he was selected to take charge of five other soldiers in a place called Avadi. This proved to be a move that met with John's approval. *"We were sort of independent there. We took our meals in the cookhouse, but that was all the association we had with the rest of the camp. An officer came over every Friday and gave us our work for the week. He brought our mail, and our pay, and also left me with a Chevrolet station wagon which we used to go to Madras on a Saturday where we wandered round this large covered place called the Moor Market."*

The work that John and his team were designated to do was to load machinery and equipment on to stationary wagons. Every two days, the loaded train would pull away for its destination, Burma, for its place to be taken by another train of flat wagons that had to be loaded with more of the large packing cases. *"It was hot; the sun reflecting off the concrete made it hotter still, so we used to start work early morning, break at mid day, and work again in the evening."* Once that work was completed, John was posted to Ceylon, now Sri Lanka, before spending some time in Burma. at a place called Chittagong. *"We were there a long long time. It was there that we heard that the war with Germany was over, but not with Japan."*

Eventually, when the war was over with the Japanese, John was sent to a holding camp in Singapore to await repatriation. *"I enjoyed Singapore"*, for the city which is now one of the major trading posts of the world was even then a busy place for dealing. John used to go in a station wagon to buy eggs, vegetables, fruit and chicken from the huge covered markets.

"I used to have a good look round, and got to know a number of the Chinese stall holders. They used to reckon up the cost of things on boards, by sliding beads along a wire, and then we paid in Straits dollars. They were always asking about CHOREY gear."

The time came to return to England to be demobbed, and John made the journey on the liner the Brittanic. *"We headed west through the Pacific into the Indian Ocean.*

Tales of a Lakeland Gypsy

We just used to laze around, gazing over the side of the boat to watch the flying fish. The sunsets were wonderful, and the stars so clear and bright, you thought you could touch them."

When he arrived back in England, and disembarked at the Liverpool docks, troop trains were waiting to take the soldiers to camps in many different parts of the country. *"Within a few days, we were throwing off our army clothes and gear to be given a common, cheap demob suit. I was given a single train ticket home, and about £80. That was all I had to show for six years in the army."*

What about all the capital raised when he was working for himself?

" That went to make the army life more bearable with all the perks that ready money could buy."

"I went in as a 19 year old boy, and I came out as a 25 year old man. Six years of my life had gone for nothing. There was no job to go to. Many of those who had been hiding at home, dodging the call up, had grabbed all the best jobs. Still my mother was glad to see me; I was back home safe and sound, but I had to start all over again from rock bottom."

John Townsley, [extreme left, back row] in PT rig!

104

Chapter Eleven

STARTING FROM SCRATCH

In spite of what he regarded as six wasted years of his life, when John Townsley returned from his military service, he was realistic enough to admit that he was one of the lucky ones. At least, he did return safely from the war, even though he only had his demob suit and £80 to show for it. The bitterness that he felt was directed towards some of those who had not been called up, and had taken advantage of the money making potential that war time, and its enforced blackout presented.

"I know that when the war was going on, there was people who dodged being called up for the forces. They started to fiddle, rob, call it what you like, the factories, works and railways. There was no one to stop them. I might say that I am one of the few left that knew what was going on. They bought anyone that got in their way; money talked all languages. They were the big money SCAMS, and I knew all of them. Some of them became regarded as pillars of society, and upholders of the law; and some of them punished other small time losers."

The fact that he had missed out on the wartime moneymaking "action" made him all the more determined to succeed in peace time, but it took him quite a while to readjust to civilian life.

One of the main difficulties that John had to face was, that in spite of all the hard grafting by the Family in the pre-war years, there was very little money left in the Family coffers. Dowries that were given to his sisters when they married had taken a substantial amount, and with no family member left at home to deal and trade, and without the support of any pension, John's mother had only survived the war years by living on her savings. There was little left. John returned home to live with his mother and set about his first priority, which was to get a job.

"I started to drive lorries for various people, and lived at home with my mother". He recalled that his working week averaged about 100 hours, for which he was paid £7. It was a hazardous job, especially in the winter. *"Then there was no salt or sand on the road, and coming over Bowes Moor from Scotch Corner was really dangerous in winter time, Today it is a doddle compared to what it used to be like. The road was narrow, about as wide as a single cart track. I have seen scores of lorries going off the road, and tumbling down onto the valley side."*

The long hours and low pay were no good to John. He didn't mind working long hours, for that was what he had been used to from a very early age; but he saw no reason why it should be for someone else's benefit. He looked for another job, and was taken on by a local man who John explained was *"very good to me, and once my work for him was done, he let me use the lorry for my sidelining; that was buying and selling."*

Tales of a Lakeland Gypsy

John's work then took him into the countryside with which he was familiar from his pre - army days, and while he was on his rounds for his employer, he was also on the lookout for sacks and rags, non ferrous metal like brass and copper that he could turn into money for himself. He started to renew and build up contacts that would be useful in selling on what he had bought.

"I got a building in the town to store my rags, woollens, metals, antiques, anything that I picked up. I got a driver from the Midlands to collect them from me. He delivered twice a week to a shoe factory in Cockermouth, and I had a man to load him up from my yard to deliver these goods to the Midlands. He was a very reliable man and I paid him well. My payment always came in cash, in a registered envelope."

In 1952 John married, and he and his wife Kath moved into a cottage opposite John's mother, who John considered to be "one of the best." Four years later, she died. *"We buried her back home, with my dad and brother Charlie, at Harrington."* This was a major loss to John, for as the youngest member of the family, he had always been especially close to his mother, but now with a wife to care for, he set about rebuilding a life for himself. He carried on driving lorries for several firms, which mainly involved lengthy journeys to London and other major cities and ports.

In this way, John earned enough money to buy his own home, and with the extra income that he made by working for himself, he was eventually able to buy his own brand new, five ton lorry. This enabled him to stop working for others, and to drive for himself. *"I used to travel all over West Cumberland and South Cumberland collecting scrap and rags. I was able to buy a bigger yard with stables and buildings which I rented. It was then that I began to get my act together."*

His first yard was in South Street, Cockermouth. The local council granted him permission to operate as a marine store dealer, and he started to extend the range of his operations beyond a merely local level. In the early days, when he was beginning to build up his business, John always drove his own lorry to collect and deliver the goods that he was trading. While he was away his wife looked after the yard. *"I let people know that I would be there after three o clock on certain days, and that way, they knew when they could come and see me about things to buy and sell".* Scrap men from as far away as Stranraer started to visit his yard, and John dropped his week day visits to farms to concentrate on his scrap metal business. *"I used to leave the yard at different times of the day when going south to do business. I got to know the men at the other end, especially the bent GADGIES. I could spot them anywhere; ROWDY was the going thing, and I always carried a roll as a straightener. I always found there was some GADGE who could be straightened by ROWDY, especially a MUSH who liked a PEEV, or a FLATTIE who liked to live above his standing. These were the ones I was always looking for."*

In the years that followed the war, the roads were not as congested with traffic as they are today. Even though there were no motorways, the quietness of the roads ensured that driving in the early hours of the morning, or late in the evening afforded relatively easy runs. John made sure his wagon was never left unattended, either on his way to deliver a load, or on the return journey home, when on occasions he carried between £8000 and £10,000 in notes, tucked into the waistband of his trousers. *"That's what I was carrying back after weighing in for the real tackle. I would phone the wife, say I had got PACIED, ready ROWDY and would be home in so many hours. I carried my own food, a piece of soap and a towel in the cab, and had a wash and freshen up while waiting for the ROWDY to be paid."*

His business grew; helped by the remnants of water time surplus equipment from military establishments, scrap clearance from rebuilding programmes, and industrial "waste" that were all there to be tapped and sold on, by anyone that had an eye for the business. The years of Family training stood John in good stead. He knew where to look; he knew who to touch; and those with things to sell knew where to come.

"This dealer from the north of the county used to go to the war surplus sales. I had done a bit of dealing with him. He came in the yard one day with a mixed load, to sell me the non ferrous metal." John recalled how he eyed up the rest of the load feigning a casual lack of interest, and then asked the dealer what he was going to do with it. There was some "light iron" which was destined for a Penrith scrap dealer where it was to be baled up into a mixed load. John upped the offer price, which the dealer was only too pleased to accept, and for the next few weeks he took delivery of a considerable amount of the "light iron." He was in no hurry to pass it on and as weeks went by, it accumulated into a substantial heap in his yard. It lay there for some time, seemingly neglected, and when the dealer paid his next visit to the yard, he asked John if he would sell it back to him; at a profit of course. He had discovered that lively bidding for similar loads of metal, at other auctions, was forcing the price up.

"Do you know what this metal is?" asked John.

"Not really" replied the dealer.

"Well I do, and have done from the beginning." John had recognised the metal as that which was used in jet engines and was noted for its remarkable heat resisting qualities. *"I had fifteen ton, and I sold it for a fantastic profit."*

As his business increased, it became obvious that his existing lorry was far too small to carry the weight of metal that was coming his way. *"I bought a new eight ton tipper with drop sides. The body was made of stainless steel. I had extra springs put in for carrying really heavy loads over the top; there was no restrictions then. I used to drive up to Scotland, leaving at ten o clock at night with five and six tons over the top. It never showed with the extra springs."*

It was rare that John returned to his yard with an empty wagon, for when travelling back from Scotland, he often brought a load of batteries, or non ferrous metal that had been collected from military camps or dealers with whom he was in contact. Most of the batteries were huge objects that had once powered submarines which, after their useful life was over, lay redundant in the Scottish naval bases. When broken open, the batteries provided a profitable source of lead which John supplied on a regular basis, to a firm of smelters in the south of England. It was as a result of battery breaking that he fell foul of a Ministry inspector.

"I had some men working for me, breaking up the batteries in an old stone quarry.

Tales of a Lakeland Gypsy

This had gone on for a long time, but one day an inspector came and told me I would have to build changing rooms and showers for the workers, and periodically the workers would have to be checked for their health. I decided against that, and the firm I delivered to said, just bring the batteries in the cases and we'll do the rest.

On occasions, deals were done during the course of the journey home. John was returning from the Midlands when he recognised a small Bedford lorry that he was following along the Thirlmere road belonged to a traveller. John signalled the driver to pull in at a lay-by, and the two men greeted each other warmly, for they were friends of long standing. Billy Buck had a load of copper, gun metal, brass and lead that he had just bought from the boat landings at Windermere

"Is t' going to buy it?" he asked John, who after giving an eye to the load, agreed and suggested that they both went to the granite quarries at Threlkeld where there was a weighbridge. *"That was the last time I saw him, although we did go to his funeral at Skipton where travellers came from far and wide."*

Although the scrap side of the Townsley business was rapidly expanding, his contacts with the farms were not forgotten altogether. John saved his farm visits for the weekend, for he was shrewd enough to realise the value of keeping in touch with folk who had proved of such value in his Family dealing days. There was still a market for barley sacks and feathers, rags and woollens, and these were easy to collect and store in one of the buildings in his yard.

Feathers were acquired as household fashions changed, and the spring interior bed became more popular than the old type feather mattresses. Housewives were only too pleased to get them out of their way, and John was only too happy to take them. He kept a special storage loft at his yard, where he separated out the pure white down KIPS that he bought from farms and country houses, from those that were filled with coarser feathers. The really top quality down beds were kept on one side, to be sold to a place in Buckingham, where he was paid a "real price". *"I sold them to a Jewish firm. They were really into feathers. They kept cages of birds, all with beautifully coloured feathers. They sold the feathers on for hats."* The lower quality feather beds were kept for an Irish dealer who used to call on a regular basis. *"These were easy to move when a truck was backed up to the building."* said John.

His wife Kathy was well able to look after that side of the business, but as John was frequently away from home, he was concerned that no metal deal should be missed, and so he trained Kath to recognise all the different types of metal. He showed her how to use the testing techniques without arousing or alerting the interest of a FLATTIE seller, so that she could buy at her price. He also taught her to appreciate the quality and value of precious metals, for his dealing also included buying high priced goods, but this was usually done by arrangement when he was at home.

He stored rags and woollens in another loft, where they were sorted into different types. Most of these were obtained through collecting on his weekend rounds, or when other dealers brought them in to the yard. Some of the rags even came from a rubbish tip. *"I was put onto a man where it was 99% legal. It was dumped by a firm onto a public tip, and this GADGE had legal access to the tip. He used to load it, take*

Tales of a Lakeland Gypsy

it to his KEN and store it in his shed, for me to collect."

As business grew, the Cockermouth yard proved too small for his needs so in order to expand he bought another yard in Workington, "for a song", which was enclosed by high walls. *"I started to operate from that yard, with a man looking after it, but brought all the valuables bought in that day home to Cockermouth at night."* With the additional storage that the new yard afforded, John bought in tremendous quantities of batteries and scrap diesel engines from trucks and buses. Some buses were bought complete for as little as £10 each. Some of these came from contracting firms where they had been used for taking men to work during the boom years. John had them stripped down and found a market for the scrap metal and the seats. Any engines that were still in good order were sold on to farmers for their machinery, or to fishermen for their boats.

In the years that followed the second world war, Workington was a busy port; boats arrived from many different parts of the world bringing raw materials for the West Cumbrian industries, and departed with finished products or coal from the West Cumbria coalfield. *"I sold lots of engines to seamen to take back to the Middle East, or Eastern Europeans; Leyland, Perkins, Bedford, Gardner were all in demand."*

Another source of aluminium that came John's way was from the debris of many wartime aircraft that crashed among the Cumbrian fells and moorlands. One fell farmer in the west of the county used to drive over his rough moorland with his tractor and trailer, to search out, and clear his land of the remains of aircraft. *"In wartime, they never really bothered to salvage all those crashed planes, and after the war there was still a lot of material lying about."*

In addition to the buses and scrap from planes, John also bought scrap metal from a major local construction firm. The post war demolition of old property, and the house building boom was a gold mine to scrap merchants, *"I used to buy loads of lead, copper pipes, tanks, back boilers, new lead off - cuts from the roofing jobs. I used to melt the clean lead, cutting it down into ingots and shoving it through to a BENT foreman for white metal. I bought the lead for about £60 a ton, and used to draw for these ingots, about once a month, for £1,600 a ton, but just FEEKING about half a ton at a time. I had to DROP to these bent GADGIES, but the return was fantastic."*

John made another profitable deal when a brewery decided to upgrade its premises and install new and improved equipment. He expressed an interest in buying the scrap metal when he was tipped off about the price tendered by another dealer. John was prepared to go just a little way "over the top". *"I had to pay for it there and then, and I was given a stamped receipt saying that all the loose scrap metal was mine. There was gun metal doors that two men couldn't lift, there was copper tanks and pipes. There was conveyer belt and chain, machinery, siphons and filter beds. I bought everything that was lying there; you are not going to believe this, but I bought it all for £25 and the GADGIE got a BUNG for himself. I led away for days. I weighed all this old fashioned non ferrous metal and scored £7,000."*

Payment among the dealing fraternity was strictly cash on the nail; any who broke their word on a deal, who cheated or didn't pay up as they promised, were blacklisted, and stored away in John's memory bank for the reckoning to be made at a later date. On occasions, the waiting time was as little as a day. *"A dealer called to buy some machinery I had in my yard. We agreed a price, but I didn't get paid on the spot. A little while later, another scrapyard man, who also wanted the machinery bid me half as much again as the first man. I told him, you can have it for cash."* The scrap dealer pulled out two large rolls of notes, and paid the price there and then. *"I also pay on the clap of the hand,"* he said. *"It's a deal"* said John, clapping the man's hand in the downward manner, and the heavy machinery was taken from John's yard that same day.

The first interested party got to hear of the deal, and came to see John some days later, but this time he was accompanied by his minder. He was aggrieved and ready to do business. *"I said, you never paid, and it's two weeks since I last saw you, and if you recall, I delivered some scrap to your yard a few years ago, and you paid £2 a ton less than the agreed price. I never forgot that."*

The man was furious, and John could see that he had come prepared for a PAGGER job, so he called up his own reinforcements from one of the yard buildings in the form of a hefty rugby playing nephew. Together, they ensured that both dealer and minder vacated the yard without too much trouble. *"We used to get FLATTIES coming to the yard trying it on, but I could FONK them yards away. We were too wide-awake for them."*

Another deal in which John was temporarily disadvantaged concerned some feather beds. After he had sold most of his existing stock to his regular Irish buyer, a local dealer turned up to see what John had left. *"If you will give me the same price that he does for the KIPS, you can have the few that's left."* The dealer agreed, and there and then made out a cheque for the required amount, which he promised to redeem for cash later on that same day when he returned from his dealings.

Sure enough, *"He called back that night with the cash, and we tore the cheque up"* said John. The dealer left with the promise that he would be back to do more business, and a few weeks later he called at the yard to collect the few KIPS that John had bought in. Once again he paid by cheque and left with the promise that he would be back to exchange the cheque for cash, as he had done before. But unlike the first occasion, he failed to return with the ready cash. The following morning, John went to the bank to cash the cheque. The bank manager laughed; *"Its lucky for you its only for £40, you will have to join the queue."* It transpired that John had been ripped off. *"He hadn't a penny piece in the bank, he was a PANCRACKER, or a social security fiddler. I had never dealt with this man before, but I vowed I would get my own back, no matter how long it took."*

This little setback didn't hinder the growth of John's business for within two years his two yards were generating such a quantity of work that he had to increase his wagon stock. *"I bought four brand new Volvo six wheelers. They were stainless steel tippers to be used for contract work, and delivering scrap all over the country."* The lorries worked round the clock, fulfilling their contract work by day and leaving the yards in the evening to travel through the night with loads of metal. *"We would load*

Tales of a Lakeland Gypsy

them up and by arrangement with the firms, and a BUNG for the GADGIE, we would tip through the night, and my drivers would be back to start work again at the quarry next morning. I used to be coming back in the early hours of the morning after delivering my own loads by special arrangement. Many a time I had a large envelope with thousands of pounds stuffed inside my shirt. Two hours from Glasgow; three and a half from Birmingham, driving a brand new six wheeler in overdrive while most of the country was asleep."

John bought off scrap dealers from all over the country as new town and city developments meant the old buildings had to make way for progress. *"Demolition contractors were pulling down old houses, pubs, churches, old mansions and there was more non ferrous metal around than had ever been known before. Lots of these metals were very old, lead, copper and gun metal was heavy gauge tackle. The old church bells that I bought were sold over again for antiques. They were digging TACKLE up from everywhere. This scrap game was DODGY. When you delivered, the workers were on the take, it affected you more if you were the owner/driver of the load. They knew you carried rolls of cash. If you could not work in with their racket, you were in queues of loaded lorries for ages. If you didn't comply with them, you could be blacklisted. If you could pay them, you jumped the queue and got paid yourself. When they got paid for services rendered, they could make your load worth a lot more money. I used to go to deliver to a few foundries that worked 24 hours. They would say, come at two or three o clock in the morning. Someone would be waiting to meet me at the weighbridge. They would say, Give me a certain amount of money, and your journey and your load will have been worthwhile. Invariably at these places, they knew you, and the BUNG game was operated. Nobody could tell what had been tipped, more so at night. Two loads for one was done by BENT weighbridge operators for cash."*

It was a common dodge to increase the value of a load by tipping a delivery of mixed metals directly on to a heap of already graded scrap. No one was able to say with any certainty what had been tipped, or indeed, how many loads had gone on to the heap. This was especially the case at night time when the favoured few were allowed to carry out their deliveries. In the darkness and bustle of a busy, round the clock, shift working steel works or foundry, it was impossible to distinguish the lower grade metals, as they poured on to the heap in a rusty, dusty cloud. The huge banks of scrap that consisted of hundreds of thousands of tons, easily absorbed another load into anonymity.

Another way to take advantage of the system, was to tip a load of scrap directly into the smelters, for in that way, the evidence of the composition of the load. vanished completely. Once again, this method of unloading a wagon of scrap was the prerogative of the favoured few dealers, who were prepared to pay on the side to the men in charge. But this also carried a special price for the metals, for there was no handling entailed.

Some of the non ferrous metals that came John's way were derived from questionable sources, but he asked no questions. Although he never asked where the metals came from, in some cases he did query its legality in his own mind. *"I had a*

.MUSHER *who used to get lots of non ferrous metals; from where, I never asked. I was introduced to him by a legal GADGIE. He left it for me at a pick up point, and he later called round for the ROWDY. He was always desperate for money. In the end, he stashed a load of jewellery, and I put some TUAVAS on. When he wanted PACIED, I said I had never seen the stuff, which was true. He left me and went to deal with some one else."*

Other metals and scrap were sold to him by the owners of companies who were on the verge of bankruptcy. *"They would phone me to come round right away; they'd had notice the accountants or bailiffs were coming in to check their stock. The goods were still their own, until they were declared bankrupt, and that was good enough for me."*

John was only too aware of the fact that there were fiddles going on against him in his own yard. When he was away, he knew that some of the men who worked for him, were "ripping him off", even though Kath was there to keep an eye on things. She also knew that fiddles were going on, but as long as the damage was not too serious, John was prepared to turn a blind eye. *"If I had sacked those workers, and taken new ones on, the new men would have just done the same."*

He was not however, prepared to ignore a deal with a big company in the north east, where he was set up to be the "fall guy." He had put in a bid of £10,000, which was accepted, for a large amount of non ferrous metal. Once John's cheque had been cleared, which was a week later, he was told he could collect his load. The lot was already bagged up, and John went to the office to get one of the bosses to supervise the load being put on to his two wagons. *"Something seemed to say to me watch what you are doing."* The first lorry was loaded with copper for which he had paid, but when they started on the second lorry, John realised that the load was "dodgy". The metals had been switched. *"I had been round too many corners and up too many streets to fall for that old trick".* He threatened to report what had happened to the firm's head office in such a strong manner, that a new and favourable price was negotiated. John came away satisfied.

"I always found there was men at the top who worked for themselves as well as for the firm. If you did not co-operate, or go along with them, they could "take you to the cleaners." Sometimes when I got back home there would be a telephone call.

"Is that you Mr Townsley?"

"Yes?"

"Well, I am sorry to have to tell you there was quite a bit of irony brass in your metals. Will you collect it when you are next down or take a lower price for it.?"

With a distance of two or three hundred miles between them, John had little opportunity to argue his case, even though he knew he had left a perfectly good load. *"So when you went to these places, you had to be prepared to play along. It was cash money they wanted, and then it was a different ball game. It was all the same, scrap, bags, rags, feathers; do it my way or be ripped off. If you went along with them, you would get permits through the post for so many delivery loads. It paid to go along with them, for they paid the best prices. That's how I found the way things were, and operated. It was like being part of the family."*

There was another bit of shady dealing that involved " the bag trade". John bought used bags from one particular factory where the manager was BENT. When John arrived at the factory, he was directed to the collection point that had been arranged with the manager, and had them loaded on to his wagon by a fork lift truck. Hidden inside the bags was a load of good quality metal. *"I used to stop at a transport cafe up the road, and he would follow in his Mercedes. He would collect what I owed him for what he had put on the lorry. I could do nothing but go along with him, or he would have said, No more loads."*

John was scornful of two other businessmen who approached him to see if he would buy all the scrap from a garage that was being refurbished. *"These two didn't know one metal from another. They came to stay in the town while the demolition took place, Like all clowns, they had a weakness for drink and women. I like these sort of people; you can use them as you like."* Among the scrap, John bought lorry loads of brass, gun metal, copper tubing, but made sure that he paid *"these two characters after each lorry load and got them to sign for the money I had paid them."*

John recalled that many of those who approached him for a deal were respected people in society; they lived in fine houses, they had responsible jobs, and some were highly regarded in the local community. But as John discovered, many were living beyond their means, and there were occasions when his phone would ring, or a knock come on his door late at night, by someone in urgent need of cash. *"I have had people from all walks of life come to me for ROWDY; even government officers and the likes with information to sell, to let me know what was going on, or something to trade."*

John found it was common practise for some owners or managers of factories, foundries and works to approach him to sell *"good clean metal by special arrangement"*. One of these was the owner of a factory who always had to be paid in cash which was sealed into an envelope and lodged in the safe of a particular hotel. *"We found he was living a double life with the lady owner and needed the extra money. His grandfather had done business with our people years ago."*

Another factory owner approached John to see if he had an unmarked van that could be left in a side street every day in the lower end of the town. *"She was a lovely lady, but the bailiffs were coming in, and until they did, she said that everything in the factory belonged to her and she wanted to get something for it."* Each morning for a week, John parked his van at the appointed place, and each evening he went to collect it, together with the best of brass that had been loaded in during the day. At the end of the week when he went to settle up, the amount came to £3000. This amount may not seem over large by today's inflated standards, but its value in 1964 is put into perspective by the tale that followed.

"I took the money up to her, she didn't live far away. She invited me in and offered me a whisky". John was hardly prepared for the next offer that was made. His client lived in a large house, a beautiful house as he described it, but as the pressure was on from the auditors and the bailiffs to recoup what they could, the lady was anxious to

realise her assets.

"Will you give me £6000 for this house?" she said

"Aye," I said, *"I can gaa down home and get it for you now."*

John went home to think about the deal and discuss it with his wife, who was reluctant to move into the house because of its isolated situation. It was a lonely place for a woman on her own. John was away from home a great deal, and the mansion backed on to a river which was raided on dark nights by salmon poachers. They decided not to go through with the deal, even though they were both aware that the house was worth much more than the £6000 asking price. *"But she needed the money. She needed to be away."*

Another works manager used to come in to deal with John every other week carrying half a ton of white metal in the boot and floor well of his car. *"I used to buy it at my own BAT. He was CHORING it out of his own business."* Other business people were prepared to ask for regular weekly payments of cash from John, in return for tipping him the wink when there was a lucrative scrap deal forthcoming. *"I found the majority of people from the top to the bottom were BENT, and prepared to try anything on for ROWDY"*

The Townsley business was not only restricted to dealing in scrap, feathers and woollens, for John appreciated there was a growing market in the antique trade, and he was often approached by his regular contacts among country and farming folk when anyone had something to sell. *"There was my old farmer friend who lived alone; he was a gambler, and he liked his whisky. He backed the horses and lost a lot of money. He often used to come to my house for company. He started off by selling me a few half and full sovereigns, then I bought some watches and chains."* As the farmer needed the cash to fuel his gambling habit, he frequently called on John and offered to sell other valuables such as paintings, clocks, silver, and even the old style £5 notes, which John referred to as "Bradburys".

"He sent for me one night to go and see something he had for sale. He brought out a small antique wooden box, about eighteen inches by ten inches. He said he would sell me the box and its contents. He opened the box and inside were bundles of the old white notes in mint condition. We counted them, and there was exactly 200 notes. There was Bradbury pound notes, and various antique notes from Scottish banks. He knew exactly what was in the box. It took us all night to check their value. He told me what he wanted, and I never bartered with him. I paid him exactly what he wanted. I never ever bartered with him, because he was a reasonable man, and I always paid his price." John bought the lot for a little above their face value, and was given a gold Albert chain, for luck. *"I took them down country to a man who was into the antique notes business and was able to sell them on for a fantastic profit."*

An old Gypsy woman who lived in West Cumbria, traded in gold. John and Kath went to do business with her and when she realised John's family name, told him, *"I know all the breed of your families"*. Her collection of gold was a veritable treasure trove, for among it were bracelets, chains, gold coins, and watches on the heavy old

Albert chains. She agreed to deal with John at the price he bid, and he continued to deal with her over many years, although he never found out where all the gold came from.

Another Gypsy lady with whom he had dealings had come to settle in Workington, and she also had a collection of gold to sell. Among the five pound pieces, fobs, and brooches, were some that John recognised as those that once belonged to his mother. *"As she was the last in line of her family, she agreed to sell them to me. She was a very nice lady, but she liked her drink, and that's how it was."*

An old dealer man from Whitehaven was a regular visitor to John's house. Invariably when he had done his dealing in gold, antiques or jewellery, and been paid by John, he would say, *"I'll just away and see if Kath has owt in t'bottle."* He liked his rum, and at the age of 80 was a *"real old character."* Kath enjoyed these visits for the old man was always full of good crack. *"He could sup a bottle o' rum or brandy while he was talking to her."* said John. One night, when John's phone rang; it was the dealer's son. *"My dad wants to see you."* he said.

The following day, John travelled over to Whitehaven to see the old man. *"He took me to see this tackle which he thought would interest me. It was old stock from a wine importer. There was Victorian furniture, pewter spirit and wine measures, crystal and cut glass bowls, antique paintings, patterned cast iron tables with claw balled feet. There was old bottles with pewter stoppers. The lot was from a business that was giving up; one of the oldest importers of rum into England. I was costing it all in my head"*

"What are you going to give me for this lot?" the old man asked.

"How much do you want" John replied. On being given the figure that was wanted, *"I bid him a few pounds less, and we had a deal. I eventually sold everything, a lot went to America; that was a real deal."*

Another "real deal" occurred when John and Kath were away on holiday in the south of England. They chanced to stop in a village where they noticed an antique shop. Their curiosity was roused by the sight of some old trap lamps displayed in the window that were offered for sale. John was tempted to buy some, and struck up a conversation with the owner of the shop who indicated that he had a great deal more in the way of horse tackle and antiques that was available for sale, but was not on display in the shop. *"He invited us to go and have a look at what he had to sell. We followed him to his home. There was all kinds of small antiques; grandfather clocks with rare faces, punch bowls, writing desks, riding crops, pewter plaques, rocking chairs, there was all sorts."* There was so much that the dealer showed John an itemised list of what was available. It had all been acquired by the dealer in response to adverts in the local paper. *"I gathered from what was said that his marriage had broken up and he was going to have out of it as much as possible."*

There was a lot of quality material that John knew he could sell without any difficulty; he was interested in a deal but only if the price was right. *"I reached a total in my head and on a piece of scrap paper, and we had a deal. I said I would pay him in notes."* A quick phone call to John's nephew was necessary to arrange for him to bring a van down to collect the antiques. Meanwhile John and Kath passed a pleasant short stay in the company of their new found dealer friend until the van arrived. *"We loaded the van using lots of old blankets for the valuables, wished the man luck, and drove back home."* Within a very short space of time, John was able to recoup his money when much of the load was sold to a Yorkshire dealer, with once again, John making a "fantastic" profit on his deal.

John stressed that in all sorts of dealings, it was, and still is, important to know the market. The contacts that he had established among dealers and travellers throughout the country enabled him to dispose of items of gold and Crown Derby pieces that came his way, especially when they had to be "moved on." One with whom John dealt, that he classed as 100% reliable was a travellerr from Berwick on Tweed. *"Buzzer had been camping at Doncaster for the St Leger. On the way back to Scotland he died. I had just sent three loads up, and would have been paid the next time Buzzer came down. His wife and brother came down, and although I had no delivery notes, I just gave Buzzer a bit extra for luck, they paid me what I was owed. I never saw them again."*

John had a reputation for being a hard, but fair dealer, and he was approached by many people with valuable things to sell for ready cash. *"All kinds of people would come, from business people who hadn't the money to open their shop on a Monday morning, to the poorest people who were struggling. They all had something to sell. Some of them were family heirlooms, others were paintings, like Thompson's before it came to light what they were worth."*

John sold his Workington yard at a good profit, to concentrate all his business activities in Cockermouth. The yards had become not only places of business, but places where old timers dropped in for a crack, where itinerants came to seek an odd day's work, or old time dealers would talk about their dealings with the Family and the Elders. The yards took on the atmosphere and ambiance of the old lonnin' in Harrington. Others who came to the yards were descendants of those who came to West Cumberland from Ireland, to seek work in what was then Campbells Steel Works. Some of these men thought it was to their greater financial benefit to sell the steel and iron, rather than make it in the hot, dirty, dusty and dangerous conditions of furnace and foundry, but in John's opinion, they were not wise to the dealing way of life. *"It was surprising how many people I came across, right down the line, were not fully WIDED."* He met and did business with all sorts of people and pronounced most of them to be DODGY. *"They would try all sorts of things on, like saying materials not up to standard, that I hadn't delivered the goods, paying so much on delivery and making you wait for months for the rest. They would make up all sorts of excuses that you didn't get your money. When I asked for it, a secretary would say, the boss is ill, yet you knew he was there all the time."*

It was vital to know the ways of the dealing game in order to survive, for John claimed that *"many of the biggest crooks never get caught. "There are all sorts of legal qualified gangsters around. I have been asked by them for real money, and they would pull strings that would be beneficial to me. I always said, when I was in the business, every FLATTIE has his price. They would come to my house, wanting money up front, for information they could pass on. I also found, if you wanted, you could make the FLATTIE judges give the verdict your way, if you were into competing in sports. Rigging is rife."*

John's business became so successful that he was able to build a large bungalow on the fringes of the Lake District National Park. It had every luxury that included a heated swimming pool and fishponds with lighted fountains, extensive rooms and large forecourts that were illuminated by floodlights. There were rose gardens and shrubberies that were all enclosed by a red brick wall. The whole complex was far removed in time and style from the home where he spent his early years, the cottage in Potters' Lonnin.'

"Yes we dealt with them all, from the lords of the manor to the poorest people. If they played it straight, they got a square deal. But for the dodgy characters, we never, ever, failed to pay them back."

Two lorries share the same registration number!

Chapter Twelve

TRIALS, TURNOUTS, TRAPS AND TACKLE

It was hardly surprising that with his Gypsy background, John Townsley maintained his interest in horses and horse drawn vehicles even when he was concentrating on building up his scrap metal business. *"I was also buying a few horses, traps and harness, and turning them over. I went to Leicester and other markets, and bought several top class traps and gigs, and sold these on to the gentry."* In some of his metal dealing transactions, he was quite happy to accept harness, turnouts, or horses themselves as part payment for anything that was owed to him, and his Cockermouth yard was rarely without a horse in one of the stables.

Although John had sold his personal share of the Townsley fish business and no longer carried on the hawking trade, he still was familiar with the contacts and connections that his family had established over many years. These enabled him to continue to deal successfully in horses, harness and traps with travellers and other country folk. His new mechanised business gave him an extra advantage, for his ventures took him further afield to buy and sell scrap, or other commodities, and thus cast a wider eye for any good horses or traps that became available for sale. *"I had a phone call one night, from way down the country from a man who made horse drawn vehicles of various types."*

This man had been recommended to John as being one who could supply a quality made vehicle. John decided to have two traps constructed to his own specifications, and agreed to send a substantial down payment for the traps. He was told they would be ready in two months. It proved to be a long two months. *"I used to phone this man often to find out if the traps were ready and was always told, Not yet. This went on for over twelve months".*

John became concerned not only for the safety of his money, but whether he would ever see the finished traps. He started questioning other dealers, and the answers he received were far from reassuring. Another trap maker warned John, *"This man is a shady dealer and trades with other people's money".* It was almost eighteen months after John had placed his order that a phone call informed him that his traps were ready.

"My nephew Howard and me went down with one of our lorries to pick them up. We got them safely loaded and tied on, and it was squaring up time. I said to the man, the time I have waited, and the money I already gave you, we will call it settled. He was annoyed, but that didn't bother me. He had not kept his word."

One of John's clients was a lady in Yorkshire who bred Welsh cobs and hunters which "she sold to the gentry". She had bought whips, harness, and other driving tackle from John, so he contacted her again to see if she was interested in buying part of a considerable amount of stock he had bought from an antique dealer in the south of the country. *"She came across that same week, with her husband, in their coach built horse box to view the items and bought the lot, apart from the one or two items that I kept back."*

There were often occasions when John was tempted to keep back one or two items for himself, and this was especially so if he came across an extra good horse, or turnout. He found it hard to resist the temptation to keep it, rather than sell it on. Always in his mind, he held the idea that he might have some personal use for either horse or trap. He was a skilled and knowledgeable horseman; after all, he had been involved with horses for as long as he could remember, and the few years he spent away from them, during his war time service, had not resulted in any loss of his expertise.

"I bought several good gigs and horse drawn vehicles, and good driving cobs which were always for sale, along with harness, riding saddles, dealer boots, and anything appertaining to horses and turnouts."

His Cockermouth yard was also the gathering ground for tips on any deals that had been recently completed, or were of interest, or even benefit, and some of them earned a slight consideration for the supplier of useful information. This followed the pattern of how much of the travellers' and dealers' gossip filtered through to the Townsley families in the Harrington lane, and in this way, John got to know from his scrap yard customers, who was ready for a touch.

One tip off about a trap recently acquired by a West Cumbrian antique dealer resulted in John finally settling an old score. This dealer owed money for some feather beds as a result of a deal that had taken place many months earlier, and John did not forget the none payment of a debt. The information that he was given about the trap came from two FLATTIE dealers who brought a load of copper and lead to be weighed in his yard one Saturday morning. While the men were chatting, one of the dealers happened to let slip that he had seen some members of a *"so called travelling family"*, working on a trap and harness to bring it to a highly polished and immaculate condition. The trap, complete with its show harness, was just parked in a street of a nearby town. The mention of such a fine looking outfit immediately aroused John's interest and curiosity, and he pressed the FLATTIE to tell him more.

"I learned in the conversation that this trap had been bought by these so called dealers from a retired mill owner who lived at Coniston. They wanted to get their money back and a bit extra, and although there had been plenty of interest shown in the trap by so called dealers and experts in antiques, not one MUSH had bid a shilling at it. They were thinking of taking it to sell at Appleby Fair, but were biting their fingers to the nails in case they were going to get owt, or if it would be left with it on their hands."

John decided to take an interest in the trap himself, and made arrangements with a HALF WIDE MUSH, to have a look at the trap on his behalf. *"I could not front it myself, because these were the ANTLE that gave me the KITE that bounced. They owed me a few pounds, nothing much to speak of, but if I showed my face, they might shy off the deal."*

The following morning, which was a grey and drizzling Sunday, John and his front man drove into the town, and while John remained hidden in his van in a quiet side street, his front man was dispatched to sound out the deal.

"Away you go and see what the score is", said John as his front man went off to inspect the trap. *"He went to feel the pulse, do you see."*

The antique dealer's family were all at home and confirmed that they did have a fine trap for sale, but as it was raining, it was safely tucked away in a garage next to the house. They were asked to pull the trap out so that it could be inspected, but were reluctant to do so because of the weather.

"How much is the business?" they were asked

No straight answer was forthcoming; the dealers explained that there were all sorts of factors to be considered. They had to take into account how much they had paid for the trap, how much time had been spent polishing it, and the number of dealers that had already shown an interest. Yet as the trap was still there, it was obvious that no firm offer had been made for it. *"Although all kinds of dealers had already been to see it, they hadn't the bottle to put a bid in"* was John's reaction. *"They could have picked it up for next to nowt."* Persistance paid off, and John's messenger eventually returned to tell him the score. *"He came down that laal narrow street, and I'm ducked down in van, keeping out of the way"*, John recalled, and was delighted to be told that it was the finest trap ever seen.

"How are they talking?" he wanted to know.

"They had paid £78 for the lot, the trap and the harness, but I think they'll want £100 for the sale." John couldn't believe his luck. Although he had the ready money available to clinch the deal right away, the owners of the trap had indicated they would not do business on a Sunday. *"We won't go past you, come back tomorrow night."*.

On Monday night, John pulled a flat wagon out of his garage, put two old hair KIPS on the back to act as cushions, or bumpers. *"I was so sure the gig and harness was as good as mine,"* he said, and arranged for one of his nephews to accompany his "front man", to clinch the deal. John drove into town separately and waited in a side street for them "to do the business". *"I didn't want to alert these people, or let them know who was behind the deal."*

He parked just out of view of where the deal was taking place, but as time went by, he couldn't contain his impatience. *"I got out, and crouched down behind the corner and just peeped down the street to see what was going on. And here's my nephew running with the trap shafts just balanced on his two hands. That's how you tell a trap, it isn't the way you put it down and lift it up; and it isn't how it goes up in the air, its balance, balance. You could balance it with your fingertips; you could pull it with your finger tips. It was that light, but strong. That's the idea of a gig, the lightness and the strength of it."*

The gig was safely loaded on to the lorry, with the help of a casual passer by, and securely tied on while the trap's harness was safely stowed away. The deal had been successfully completed. *"I thought this is BARRIE. What a touch. I could have sold the trap that night to a client for £3,000."*

Exhilarated by his success of at long last getting even with the family that had cheated him, John decided that the deal called for a celebration, and a final settlement of finances at a local pub, "The Lime Kiln".

"What's the deal?"
"£100 and three pounds back for luck."
"What do you want for your corner?"
"The three quid will do me"

It was inevitable in the close world of dealing that John's coup would come to light. *"When they found out who had set up the deal, they were dumbfounded. I had waited for the feather bed FLATS and I had closed the net on them. I had waited a long time for that day. I had got my money back hundreds of times over, and I let them know they were out of their depth in these sorts of deals."* The fact that John never forgot anyone who let him down on a deal, and invariably caught up with them, sooner or later, had paid off yet again.

His newly acquired trap was of such excellent quality that John kept it for his own use. *"It was a back to back gig, made of pure mahogany with beautiful lancewood bent shafts with brass fittings. What a machine. The harness was chromed leather, piped along the edges with linseed to keep it supple. It had been specially made. The rubber tyres were as good as new; it had hardly been used."*

Although the increased ownership of motor cars by country folk ensured that driving traps and gigs went out of general use, there was and still is, tremendous enthusiasm for carriage driving as a competitive event at trials and shows throughout the country. Initially, John drove his newly acquired trap round the lanes and bridle ways of Cockermouth just for his own pleasure, but eventually his interest in driving took on a competitive edge as he joined other enthusiasts who took part in a number of events. The standard of driving competitions in which he became involved ranged from that found at local shows such as Loweswater, to the prestigious national event that takes place at Lowther Park, and which for some years counts HRH, the Duke of Edinburgh, as one of the competitors. John realised that his newly acquired mahogany gig, was ideal for these events, but it needed the right horse to pull it, if it was to be of any use in competitions. It was the acquisition of a Welsh cob that enabled John to be in a position to take on the best.

"I won all over with this gig and harness, with the real chestnut cob between the shafts. I won the Lowther Driving Trials in 1977, competing against the so called best in Britain, over three days. I reckon I put the lot of them in the shade. We won at a canter, for no one had seen a cob like mine at Lowther before."

John trained his cob in the old Gypsy way with plenty of road work. That ensured the horse was *"muscled up"* and fit enough to tackle the different disciplines of dressage, obstacle and cross country courses, that made rigorous demands on both horse and driver.

"We won a silver cup for that, but I had to pay to have my name engraved on it"

121

he wryly commented.

The cob was called James, which John bought as a two year old, and claimed it was the best cob that ever came out of Wales. *"I gave £650 for it with his registered papers. He was 14.2 hands, chestnut with a flaxen mane and tail. He had four white socks with good feathers. He was a stallion so I decided to have him registered."*

Registration involves a combination of paper work and veterinary inspection. The required fee was sent to the appropriate Government department and John was notified that in due course a government veterinary inspector would check the horse over. It was a busy Monday market day in Cockermouth when the veterinary came to inspect James. John's stables and yard then formed part of the larger auction market yard, and attracted a knowledgeable and interested crowd of spectators to watch the vetting.

"There were farmers, horsy people and holiday makers all interested in what was going on." said John. His nephew, Howard Burns, who was a young lad at the time, and a natural and skilled horseman, was on hand to help out with the vetting.

"The vet said to my nephew, jump on him and ride him for five or six miles then bring him back to the stables."

After the workout, the vetting started in earnest.

"He went all over the animal in detail and then told Howard to jump on the horse's back and trot him in the yard. He was watching the action and movements. Jump down, twist him round, and round, turn the other way, and all the time he was watching."

There followed another hands on check before Howard was sent away again with the horse.

"Make him back, bring him forward, run him away in hand, bring him back again." After more checks, John was delighted to be told that he would get the necessary registration documents and that in the vet's opinion, the cob he had submitted for examination was the best that he had ever seen.

Word got round about the quality of the horse. *"I had vets, horsy people, even people from racing stables come to see Howard show the horse off. He could ride him in and out of traffic with just a halter, or bareback at speed down Station Street. In the yard, James, would follow him like a dog. We timed him several times over a measured mile on a straight road in a spindle backed gig. He could do it in just over two minutes. Howard used to ride him along the old railway track, jumping fences and five barred gates like a stag. He loved to go in a deep pool of the Cocker salmon river, called the Black Hole. Howard would dive in and the horse would follow. This horse loved the water."*

With the combination of James and the mahogany gig, John had winning results at other nationally recognised events such as Holker Hall, Cark in Cartmel, and more northern venues, where he had the satisfaction of beating the world carriage driving champion at that time, another Cumbrian man, George Bowman. The success of James at these events earned that chestnut cob recognition as "The Cob of the North".

Tales of a Lakeland Gypsy

On other occasions, if John was not competing with his own turnout, he drove in events for other owners. *"I won Keswick with one of George Bowman's horses. George was abroad at the time and he wanted to try out one of his team of four in hand chestnut cobs. That team and a four wheeler was eventually bought by Bristow, the helicopter millionaire. You meet a lot of nice people in the driving game."*

After winning at Keswick Show, with James and his favourite mahogany trap on August Bank Holiday Monday, 1977, John never bothered to drive in competition again.

"A gentry lady wanted to buy the complete turnout for any sort of money, but I said, No. I just drove for pleasure after that around my home town of Cockermouth. People were always coming to the stables to see him, or lighting up the town as I drove him through the streets. Many people had never seen anything like it before."

James stayed with John for a further two years and was then sold to a stud farm in Kent. *"I was giving my business up then, things were changing, the stables were going, so I saw he had a good home to go to."* He also reflected how the influx of sponsorship into the sport has made life easier for those competitors fortunate enough to catch the eye of a sponsor. *"Today, some of them have their horses bought for them as well as the harness and all the tackle. Some even have special motorised horse boxes so they can travel about to the shows in comfort, and some are able to compete abroad at the sponsor's expense."*

The winning turnout of horse, trap and harness that had cost John a total of £750, was recouped for many thousands of pounds, when he eventually sold the trap and harness, with a different Welsh cob, to a local landowner, who lived with her husband, a wealthy industrialist in a large house on their estate in the Cockermouth area. John described her as a *"proper, proper lady"*. His first meeting with her took place when John was competing in a driving event at Hesket Show. She approached John to have a chat about driving.

"She was wanting to get into the driving game. We talked and talked and she said I'll come and see you in your yard at Cockermouth. She was a marvellous horse-woman, she used to ride with the Cumberland Foxhounds."

Some time later, she visited John's yard, *"She bought traps and sets and sets of brand new harness I had specially made in London. She bought gigs and all kinds of tackle, and I sold her that mahogany trap and the brown leather harness with another Welsh cob. That Welsh cob was another good horse. He was called Prince, he won the Royal Highland Show at Edinburgh. He was a good un', he could be driven by a child. I told her that I could guarantee Prince anywhere, because he is bombproof, he is so quiet."*

Prince responded well to his new driver on the trial run in a trap around Cockermouth. The deal was made, and John had another satisfied customer, for Prince went on to win every driving event in which he was entered. Evidence of Prince's placid nature later became evident as a result of a tragic event that occurred when his new owner was driving him between Caldbeck and Sunderland.

"She was just by herself in the trap on a lovely summer's day, and she had a heart

123

attack. There was an open gate in the lane, it was wide open, for the farmers were in the field making hay. And that horse he just pulled right in through the gate and just started eating hay. The farmer came up and they found her in the gig, but she was gone. She was a real lady."

John had established a reputation for being able to supply good quality horses to satisfy what he classed as quality people. He felt that his position was regarded with jealousy by some of the other local dealers who did not seem to get the lucrative deals that were coming his way. In his opinion, some of those who operated in the closed world of horse dealing tried to put off John's potential customers through implying that there were faults in the horses. *"They dropped a word here, or a hint there, but it didn't work. People could see for themselves that I had good horses, and I had a good reputation for fair dealing with the people that came to my yard."*

One day, John received a phone call from the owner of a large mansion house in South Cumbria where extensive roof and guttering repairs had resulted in the need to dispose of a large quantity of scrap lead. It was a deal in which John was interested, so he went to inspect the scrap and negotiate a price for the lead. When that deal was concluded to everyone's satisfaction, the owner showed John some horse tackle that included some whips. Quickly he realised their sales potential and was only too happy to make an offer for them, which was accepted. *"They were antique German Muller whips. They were still wrapped up in their original packing paper and cardboard; they were a gift."*

The selling of horse tackle formed an important side line to John's main scrap business. *"I sold lots of sets of harness, whips, carriage lamps as well as different kinds of traps. I had quite a good turnover as lots of people were become interested in driving and were just starting up."*

Two Gypsy lads, that John had known for years came into his stables to have a look at the horses. They were invited round for SCRAN and over the meal, they sounded out the possibility of buying a grey gelding.

"Do you ever yoke him in harness?"

"Yes, would you like to see him doing the business?"

Bob, the grey was yoked up, and when the two Gypsy lads climbed aboard, John was asked to demonstrate what the horse could do. *"I let him go through the town, which was very busy. We drove through the stalls in the market, there was just room to get through, then it was back into the town, and out of town again for a couple of miles where I really let him have his head."*

They returned to the yard to do business.

"How much is he John?"

"I said £1200, they bid me £800 but I refused. I later sold him to a farmer, for his daughters, but drew him back when they lost interest. Then I sold him on to a driving school in the south of England who used to train people in horse driving skills, and made good money on both deals."

Tales of a Lakeland Gypsy

One year when John was on holiday in the west country with his wife Kath, they took the opportunity to call at the "Horse and Vehicle Sale " that is held three or four times every year at Reading. This prestigious event attracts those people who are interested and involved with horses, from all walks of life.

"It would be about 1978, and I was toying with the idea of getting another gig. We were looking around before the sale started, and I got talking to this lady and her son. She was looking out for a 2 wheeler for driving a tandem pair. We were both looking at the same trap, and this lady, and she was a lady, asked if I was interested in it. She had even brought one of the joiners from her estate to check the woodwork to make sure that it was sound. I told her about Lowther."

They talked for a while, then the lady moved on to look at some other traps.

"I said to the lad, What does your dad do, son? He said he works in the City, we have estates in Oxfordshire and Leicestershire. My mother is Lady C -".

Later in the day, John resumed his acquaintance with her ladyship. *"They were very wealthy people and seeing that I was interested in Welsh cobs, and had won a lot of events, we were invited to call at her Manor House after the sale to see her collection of vehicles, and her Welsh cobs. She told me if I didn't get a gig, I could borrow one of hers to use at Lowther, and take it back to her at my convenience."*

In spite of the differences between their two different cultures and family background, John found plenty of common interests to share with a fellow competitor whose last event had been taking part in the driving trials at Windsor, and who, after giving up active competition, became a judge. On his return journey, John accepted the invitation to visit her home.

"The Manor House was out of this world, and those stables, Oooh, it was a proper spot. And she took us at face value; she was a thorough, thorough lady; no airs and graces, and you know, I've never forgotten her."

John looks back over his seventy years experience with horses and horse drawn vehicles, and conjured out of his memory recollections of all the different types that were used.

"All kinds of different carts were used. There were four wheeled drays; these were the heavy type that were built to be pulled by the heavy horses like the Clydesdales that were used by coal merchants. There was lighter four wheeled types like drays, platform, or van types that gave protection to goods in bad weather. Flat carts were mostly built in Bingley in Yorkshire and I remember coming across a Bingley cart in the south of England that had my grandfather's name on it. There were landaus, phaetons, tandem gigs, high perch, skeleton gigs, all painted and well built to high standards. Even the Councils had their turnouts for road making and sanitary work."

John's own driving days may now be over, but the memories are there in the photographs that record his achievements.

The winning combination. John Townsley, Howard Burns and the Welsh cob James. Keswick 1977.

John Townsley, Howard Burns, and Bob in the Auction Yard, Cockermouth.

Chapter Thirteen

APPLEBY FAIR

Appleby Fair is one of the traditional gatherings of travelling folk. Although the event is still regarded as part of the true Gypsy calendar, as the years progress, their numbers are swelled by others who, without the background of a Gypsy heritage, have nevertheless taken to the itinerant way of life. *"When I was a boy I used to go to Appleby Fair. The leading travelling people all used to meet there. They had their own lot on the grass verge, which was theirs for decades."*

In John's opinion, Appleby is now a sham of its former self. While he is aware that there are still some of whom he regards as the genuine travellers, who continue to meet up there, he feels the majority are what he describes as MISFITS and PANCRACKERS. *"What a come down to what it used to be. It has destroyed itself. You just have to weigh up the picture, and you automatically come to your own decision,"* he reflected. On one occasion when John visited the fair, he was hailed by a traveller, though not in recognition; *"A woman shouted out to me, I will tell you your fortune sir. "I said, You're a bit late dear; my people were DUCKERING on this fair hundreds of years ago."*

Appleby Fair, which was formerly a two day event, is now spread over five days in June, and takes place on the outskirts of the market town, which still retains its old county affinity in the name of Appleby - in - Westmorland. The traditional day for selling horses is the second Wednesday of the month, but other events have been added to the Fair, to make it an extended period of Gypsy gathering. Colourful stalls sell china and silver; gold jewellery attracts a crowd. There are plastic buckets and cuddly toys, gleaming harness and painted pictures. Hot dog vans waft their onion smells to the waiting queue at the ice cream vans, and titillate the taste buds of the crowds that gather for Appleby Fair.

The Fair has been held for over 300 years since a charter was granted by James II in 1685. This original charter bore no mention of horse trading, but as horses were required for so many aspects of everyday life, it is almost certain that dealing actually did take place. Over the latter years of this century, as the need for horses for working purposes has declined, the composition of the travelling population that gathers at Appleby has changed, and that combined with a reduction in the number of genuine Gypsy families who attend, has provoked suggestions on more than one occasion, that the Fair should be stopped. But in spite of objections from some, the Fair carries on, although now it is held a little distance from the town centre to reduce the risk of damage to property in the town. It is held on the outskirts of Appleby. Yet like a magnet, it still draws travellers from all over the country. They converge on what was once

Tales of a Lakeland Gypsy

Gallows Hill, and there, make their temporary home for the duration of the Fair. At the time of the Royal Charter, Gallows Hill was outside the town boundary, and so trading took place within the town itself.

It is a triumph for tradition that the Fair still survives, for there have been a number of attempts to have it stopped. Although the camping and trading has now been moved well away from the town centre, the travellers have been allowed to continue the custom of washing their horses in the river Eden that flows alongside the town. As a sign of modern times, the debris of discarded plastic bottles of washing up liquid, whose contents served as equine shampoo, float in a gaudy flotilla on the river Eden. Recklessness in driving the horses into the river occasionally brings tragedy, for in 1995 a traveller was successfully prosecuted for inflicting cruelty on a horse when the animal drowned in the river.

From a distance, the sight of closely packed wagons, parked up on the Appleby hillside, is an impressive and colourful array. The green canvas hoods of the wooden painted, traditional style Gypsy caravans, stand beside sleek white and chrome monster living vans. Yet, as one gets closer, there appears to be an order of sorts in their arrangement. Groups of vans cluster together; close to a circle of charred earth and grey ash, which hint of the romantic notion of Gypsy life, when one can imagine swarthy faces aglow in the flickering flames of a camp fire. Realistically, it is probably nothing more than the cold remainder of last night's barbecue, as old traditions are exchanged for modern trends.

But there are old timers to be found among the wagons that are far removed from the hustle of the trading and dealing that is going on along side the road where horses are trotted for inspection by potential buyers. An Elder who sat on the step of his living van had the company of three of his six sons. Two of them were tall and tanned; the skin of their faces and arms was the colour of rich mahogany. They were well made young men; the third was a youngster, still to grow. The Elder's five daughters were away among the crowds, dressed in their finery to enjoy the day. We chatted as he proudly pointed out the intricate hand painting on his traditional van. that had been done by one of his sons. The talk was sociable and friendly, echoing the warmth of the June sunshine as we sat in the shelter of the vans.

Many other vans stood quiet and empty, as their owners enjoyed the liveliness of the fair. The only sign of life was in the Gypsy security system, where each van was guarded by a chained lurcher. Some dogs lay silent, stretched out in the heat of the day, others lazily lifted a head to open an eye of curiosity. Those, who were more alert in the shade of a van side, prowled to their chain's length, and barked a warning.

Round and behind another group of vans, a dark eyed child stared with curiosity. He was no taller than the carpet lined, make shift dog kennel, that stood beside his home. The boy stared, his solemn expression gave away no secret, as he clutched a three month old puppy tightly in his arms. The animal showed no distress; the two seemed good companions. Beside the kennel, a bantam scratched at five day old powdered earth, within the confines of its wired home. The question arose, is it kept for its eggs, or the pot? There were no words of response, just smiles; and his of apprehension.

Loud and sweet was the bird song that drew attention to another van, where seven small wooden cages lined a bench that extended for half the length of the exterior of a gleaming caravan. Each held a small bird. Goldfinches were there, zebra finches, and some cross breds, but all chirruped brightly in the sun as they ritualistically hopped from perch to floor and back again. The van door was open, and a friendly invitation was given to join the two women occupants in a cup of tea or a cold drink. They displayed a courteous hospitality as we chatted about the travellers. They had made the long journey from the south of England especially to come to the Fair, and there they would return, once the Fair was over.

There were lorries full of scrap, alongside which industrial oxygen cylinders lined up in regimented rows; there was a jumble of cutting and welding gear that told of a Gypsy's trade, and tangles of harness tackle. Lorries with tarmac adverts blazoned along the side, mingled with the tethered ponies and goats. My steps led to a magnificent large and luxurious van. Inside, the white fitted furniture, gold lined, and spotlessly clean, held cabinets of exquisite china and crystal. The cushions were sumptiously thick. The owner claimed to be a millionaire but he sat upon the floor of his van in the deep pile of a spotless cream carpet

From the Hill, the road drops down to Appleby. Alongside the grass verges skewbald and piebald horses were tethered to the wire fence. Some had their young foals, which were still tottery on spindly legs. Their dark eyes were wide, with a similar apprehensive stare as that of the Gypsy child. The sight of these young and vulnerable animals, that were offered for sale, evoked a sentimental chorus of oohs and aahs from soft hearted visitors.

On the banked verge opposite the horses, scattered groups of men lazed in the sun, watching the huddle of buyers and sellers across the road. There was something slightly incongruous about one dealer who suddenly turned away from a potential buyer to use his mobile phone. To what purpose remained a mystery, but modern technology seemed intrusive in such a setting. Every now and again, the dealings were interrupted by a clatter of hooves as a horse and trap was driven along the road for the trotting area.

Here the road was closed to traffic, for along its length, and overlooked by some of the parked Reading caravans, were carts and traps being driven at a furious pace, as Gypsy men showed off their horses to any potential buyer. Among the crowd of check shirted, casually clad traders, and the colourful summer dressed visitors, were three blue shirted RSPCA officers. They were looking for signs of ill treatment among the horses, dogs and other animals that were offered for sale, or waiting an owner's return.

"It's difficult to find out who an animal belongs to. If we come across one with an injury, we get it treated by a vet. If we ask about, to find out who is the owner, we just get a shrug. Sometimes, one of the genuine Gypsies, who really care about their animals, will come up and quietly tip us off. There's something down there I think you should have a look at, they'll say."

Tales of a Lakeland Gypsy

But it's not only the Gypsies' animals that need a watchful eye, for in some of the cars of visitors to the Fair, dogs have been left behind to suffer the sweltering heat. These incidents have also to be investigated.

There seems to be a policy of turning a blind eye to some of the less serious offences that go on at Appleby Fair. *"There are so few of us, and so many of them"* explained one Inspector. *"The police try to keep the lid on things to stop any serious violence boiling over"*, was one reason given. *"If a none traveller, in their every day lives, was doing some of the things that go on here, they would fall foul of the law"*. Out of date tax discs, or none at all are commonplace on the parked vehicles on the Hill, which indicated the differing attitudes that many travellers hold in their view of the law.

In a gateway to a field, a woman stood behind a wooden table where caged birds were offered for sale. Cock goldfinches in their bright breeding plumage made a colourful show. *"Twenty five pounds each"* was the answer to a query of how much the woman was asking.

Was she a traveller, or a FLATTY trying to cash in on the travellers delight in these small, caged birds? None showed the legally demanded closed leg ring, required by the Wildlife and Countryside Act of 1981, that allow these birds to be legally offered for sale.

Loud shouts warned of the approach of a galloping horse. This is not the place to wander witless along the road. Clattering hooves skidded as a horse struggled to keep its feet on the smooth tarmac surface. Foam dripped from its mouth; its nostrils flared wide, and its eyes had a wild look. The driver leaned back in his seat, leather reins wrapped tautly about his fists, legs outstretched, as with a flash of his red shirt he whirled past, to the whoops and encouraging howls from alongside the road.

A small shire horse was led into the road, with its handler keeping a firm hold on the rope halter. It clattered along, the hair of its cream mane and fetlocks rose and fell with each high step. They contrasted beautifully with its fawn and cream dappled body as it trotted at a steady pace along the road. A stocky man in grey-brown tweeds ran behind, lashing a whip across its rump; he grinned at the watching crowd. Another lash, another grin that seemed to indicate his self assurance in his macho image, for the lash appeared to be of little purpose. The horse was returned to its tether on the grass verge where it seemed none the worse for its whipping up the road. A knot of other tweed suited figures clustered round the group of brown and white horses of which the dapple was a part. Bundles of grubby notes were counted; hands were slapped, and a deal was done.

John Townsley believes that of all the travellers that now come to deal at Appleby Fair, only a small percentage can trace their family history to the true Gypsy people who swept over western Europe in great waves from the east. The presence of Gypsy people was first documented in England and Scotland in the 16th century, when their fearsome appearance was the cause of considerable alarm. They were first recorded in Scotland in 1504, and it is reputed that the name Little Egyptians, was abbreviated to become Gypsies. In John's opinion, the greater percentage of those who now come to the Fair, are what he calls DIDECOTS or PITMEN, or FLATTIES trying to be true travellers.

"There are a lot of misfits or hipps who follow these fairs and give them bad publicity. A lot of them are out for anything that doesn't include the old ways of dealing. Many of them are just low life drop outs that know all about scrounging, and not much about work."

John has no time for the travellers who create controversy about camping grounds for Gypsies. *"There is still a problem all over the country about where Gypsies can, and cannot camp. There is a BREED that has made it worse for all travellers with the filth they leave behind, and the damage they do. Most of these people are not connected to the true travellers. They are just dyke back people who know their way to the PANCRACK office. The numbers of these people are swelling, and when they are stopped by the authorities for making a nuisance, or moved on, they say we are travelling people. Luckily, most of these dropouts are in the south, and they have the audacity to say, We want camping grounds. Many of them are just dirty, idle people of FLATTY origin. The real old, pure bred travellers respect the countryside, and work hard to provide for themselves".*

This poor image of the present day Gypsy, may be one reason why many members of once notable Gypsy families no longer want to be reminded of their heritage. *"When you go to the horse sales where people are buying and selling real class horses, some of the people want to forget the title of Gypsy or traveller. They have started to call themselves business men."* Others however, still cling to the tradition of the true Gypsy, proud of their heritage, who can still speak in Romany or Cant. *"My people, who live all over the English speaking world can converse in Romany or Cant. They do this so they don't include outsiders. It is still used in business deals to keep them private."*

As travel becomes easier, and people emigrate to spread all over the world, a number become interested in the possibility that they too may have Gypsy blood in their veins. *"We have had people from all over the world wanting to know if being called Lowther or Townsley meant that they are Gypsy bred; some regard it as an honour to be part of an old family's history."*

John explained his own attitude towards being a member of a Gypsy family in the present day.

"My people never wanted to be anything other than what they are; white faced Gypsies. We've kept our feet on the floor. If I can get a crack with a man, like myself, a Gypsy, about the ways of life in the past, and not so much of the present, that to me is history. Its about my family and my people, and for me, there's nothing to compare with it. I think I am just fortunate to have seen part of the old days."

Washing down a horse in the river Eden, Appleby.

Showing off its paces, Appleby Fair.

Chapter Fourteen

THE CANADIAN CONNECTION

Many of the people who left the British Isles to seek a new life in North America were forced to do so following the hard times that were brought about by the potato famine in Ireland, and the clearance of crofting communities in the highland regions of Scotland. Other adventurous folk sought the chance to create a new life filled with greater opportunities than they could find at home, following the trauma of the first world war. There were those who sought to escape from the consequences of their actions, and took refuge in a new country where there was space to lose themselves in anonymity, and less likelihood of awkward questions being asked.

From countries with a highly structured class system, the newly developing country presented a chance for those with ability, but without position of rank or class, to succeed. In modern terminology, they started on a level playing field, where the criteria for success was not through belonging to a privileged hierarchy, but a determination to succeed through natural ability allied to a capacity for hard work.

Some members of the Townsley family were among those who took this opportunity in North America, and went on to eventually build a powerful and influential family dynasty, based on sharply honed dealing skills that were second nature to them. The earliest members of the Townsley family to settle in Canada travelled across the Atlantic in the early 1800's. Tales that have been handed back down through the family indicate how easily they were able to make a living as long as they carried on working in their traditional Gypsy way.

"They could adapt to anything to make money. It was a new country, but they carried on with the old ways they had learned in England. That was varying the art of good traveller know how. It was just routine to them. They hawked and moved on with their horse drawn vans, and built up their money so that in later years their families were able to get mechanised. Yes these people were real pioneers. The families and their descendants that are out there now, have definitely got to thank the old 'uns for making the way for them, and putting down a really solid base for them to have a really good life."

John's closest relative to begin a new life in Canada was his brother, Charlie who sailed across the Atlantic with two of his cousins, Tom and Jamesy. These were sons of "Big Charlie" who lived in the neighbouring cottage down Potters Lonnin. *"The cousins were more like brothers"* said John who was many years younger than his own brother Charlie. *"Where one went, the others went; they went to school together; they grafted together. Tom was one hell of a smart, clever operator. So were the other two boys, Charlie and Jamesy, but Tom was a lad that had a go, and was a daredevil after being in the first world war. The MUSKER often came after him, the black curly haired one, but he was too clever for them; he was always covered."*

When the three lads went out to Canada, they first stayed with some relatives in Montreal, but it was not long before they were able to make a living for themselves, for they started to work almost as soon as they landed. With their background of country skills, they were able to take advantage of the wealth of natural resources that was freely available to them in the countryside, and there for the taking. *"They started making baskets; at least, two made them, and one went out selling them in London Ontario. They stuck to that for the first winter, then they started to get itchy feet and began moving around."*

There was plenty of wilderness country for the lads to exploit, where they could virtually live off the land. Their years of training with the families ensured that they could turn their hands to virtually any task that earned them money. *"They could adapt to any kind of hawking, dealing, horse trading, because they had done it all before. They went right across Canada and back Other traveller were amazed at how versatile they were"*. The three cousins, who were all young men in their early twenties, travelled about in their old Ford car, which was one of their earliest, but most essential, purchases. Loaded with their hawking tackle and the tent in which the three young men slept, crammed with pots and pans and other hawking tackle, the little car was under pressure day after day.

The lads were mechanically minded, and thus were able to keep the vehicle on the road, in spite of many temporary breakdowns, but on one occasion, even their combined skills could not rectify the fault. The nature of the problem was serious enough for them, to seek help from a garage.

"They needed a special part to repair it, and they were in a remote place. So they took it to this two bit garage. While the GADGE was repairing their car, the lads were MANGING saying, We will CHUCKY him NASH, which meant they wouldn't pay the GADGE"

However, the lads who had taken refuge in their Gypsy language of Cant, to decide a way to avoid paying for the job, were amazed to find that their so called GADGE was not only listening to them, but actually understood what they were talking about. *"He was one of the same BREED. His people had originally emigrated from Scotland to Canada, so the clan met up again."* Needless to say, this was one GADGE that wasn't taken for a ride by the lads.

It was almost inevitable that the life-style they practised ensured that they met up with other travelling folk in, and around the Canadian city of Montreal. They quickly discovered that it was a good city for hawking SWAG from the warehouses. Lots of merchandise came directly into the city by boat, and some of it found its way via the warehouses into the city shops, or the Townsleys hawking packs. It was while John's brother Charlie was selling Irish linen round the doors of some of the more affluent parts of the city, that he had a surprise. When he knocked at the door of one house, it was opened by a man who appeared to be a mirror image of himself.

"They were the doubles of each other; they were as alike as two peas in a pod. The

man who opened the door was a doctor, and he was called Townsley."

When the lads found trade was good in an area, they settled in that place for a reasonable length of time, and this enabled them to be keep in touch with what was going on at home. *"My mother used to send the weekly paper out with cigarettes wrapped inside it,"* said John. After a few years of skilful dealing, allied to shrewd judgement, and their ability to do any job at any time, the BOYS became so successfully established in their new country that they were in a position to help other relatives when the need was there.

" They used to get telegrams and telephone calls from travelling people in England to see if they could help them get started. The Townsleys used to say, Canada is a large country, big enough for them all to come over to get a living."

One of John's cousins who emigrated along with his elder brother Charlie, was Tom Townsley, son of Big Charlie. However, Tom was not one to stay in Canada all the year round, for he used to travel backwards and forwards across the Atlantic in the days when the sea crossing was measured in weeks rather than days, and before commuting became fashionable. He returned to England for the winter time, and when the longer days of spring beckoned, he knew it was time for him to go back to Canada, the country in which he made a fortune.

John recalled the affection and respect that Tom had for Mother Ellen. *"He used to say I have travelled and met all kinds of WIDE ANTLE, but I have never met the man or woman who could be compared with my Aunt Ellen Townsley."*

Jamesy Townsley was another of John's cousins who succeeded in making his fortune in America. *"Jamesy is dead now, but his family are carrying on with all sorts of businesses. Jamesy was the most travelled of all travellers, With his family they trucked and traded from Alaska to Mexico, in every province of Canada and every state of the USA. They also worked through New Zealand and Australia."*

The third member of the trio to emigrate was John's brother Charlie. He was denied the fortune making success of his cousins for he was summoned back home to help run the family business in England when his father became ill. Sadly, Charlie died as a young man.

Some other of John's relatives were members of a family called Winter, who settled to live in London, Ontario. *"The Winters were Scottish travellers, who originally came from the Dalkeith area. One old man told me how, in the early days when they were travelling about Canada with a horse drawn wagon, they were caught by severe conditions of cold and snow. They thought they were "goners", but the North West Mounted Police came to their aid, just as they thought that they were doomed."*

Marriage by Townsley girls brought closer ties with the Winter family. *"They were the king pins among the dealers in the area round London, Ontario. They were into every type of dealing, and also buying and selling property and land. They owned a block of shops on the main DRAG in Ontario."*

The block of shops which they owned afforded the opportunity to trade in all manner of goods that included Irish linen, antiques, rugs and furniture. Shrewdly they concentrated on the basic requirements that people needed to set up, and replenish their homes. With the success that they achieved, they tried to persuade other members of their extensive family back in England and Scotland to join them in the fast growing and comparatively young country. It was even suggested to John's family that the houses, yards and buildings should be YAGGED for insurance purposes so that the Families could start afresh in Canada. But John's family refused to leave, and instead appreciated the presents that the Winters sent over for them, or brought when they came back home to visit their relatives.

"They used to send us hampers by sea, and all kinds of clothes for the men and women that included fur and astrakhan coats. They sent shoes with elastic sides that were made of leather and these were for men, women and children. Some of the boots for the women had buttons all the way up the sides. When they came over by sea, they docked at Liverpool, and sent on all the luggage that was delivered to our houses down the lane. They brought leathers and suedes. These Winters were wealthy travellers in those days, having several money making businesses."

Some of John's North American relatives have come a long way since the early trading days, when their forefathers lived in a tent and drove round the country seeking work in a battered old Ford car. Now, their affluent life style enables them to live in comfort and luxury that is provided by trailer parks, which they own and manage all over Canada and the USA.

"The trailer parks that the Townsleys own, include some that have their own private water supply. They have swimming pools and ballrooms, large bars and clubs where the entertainment includes singing the old English songs as well as country and western. Nearby are the offices of their trading ground with sales of lots of luxurious long wheel based trailers that are gorgeously painted to individual designs. They sell automobiles, pickups, jeeps and trucks, and the men and women trade in new tackle SWAG of all descriptions."

John's cousin Tom who made such a success of his life died over 50 years ago, but the business is carried on by his son Tom who owns a trailer park in Fort Myers, Florida, which he and his family use as a retreat from the rigours of the Canadian winter. Once the weather improves, they return north to personally resume the management of their businesses in Ontario and Calgary for the Canadian summer.

For many of the Canadian Townsleys, it is summer all the year round.

Many years ago, two members of the Townsley family found that their road to success started not in the heat of a North American summer, but in the icy wastes of the Himalayas. The tale that John told is one that was often repeated among members of his family as they sat round the fire in his home down the Harrington lane.

"Two of the lads, now long gone, deserted the army while they were in India. They ran and walked across the foothills of the Himalayas and the Hindu Kush to get clear away from their regiment. On the way, they were befriended by natives who gave them food and shelter. They made their way to a port and got on a cargo boat to come home, but they couldn't stay in this country because they were wanted men, so they had to

Tales of a Lakeland Gypsy

move on. They sailed to Canada on a boat. Of course, the present members of the families are Canadians and Americans now, but they have not forgotten their roots." They gradually built up their businesses by travelling round farms and houses to sell every day goods that were needed in a scattered community. As they prospered, so they developed warehouses where they could stock all sorts of household goods which they supplied to local stores as well as to individual customers. They also traded in horses, and even today, are able to carry on this trade with people who work the land in the old way.

"There are some people in North America called the Armenians, and when they buy a farm and work the land they use horse power only. They are very good farmers and my people are able to do a lot of business with these people."

Old ways die hard, and many of the Clan, as John calls them do a lot of "top class DUCKERING," that's fortune telling to the ordinary American folk. Much of it is done on the appointment system, and as might be expected in what is still regarded as the land of opportunity, there are many people who are anxious to know whether that opportunity will actually come their way.

A number of the women still find that they are drawn to the hawking way of life, but whereas in the old days, and in the old country they would have sold second hand clothes from a trap, in the fashion conscious climate of America today, it is top class clothes, leather goods, bags and silks that are sold from the boot of a limousine.

One travelling man who has built up a business for himself on the American border, near Detroit has a factory where he employs a large number of workers to make the luxury caravans that are so popular as trailer homes for Canadians and Americans, who like to enjoy the the advantages and greater freedom of an open air life-style. Some of John's north American relatives live permanently in these luxurious trailers, and make a living by buying and selling this type of vehicle, and will, if the need arises, sometimes actually sell off the trailer affixed to the tow bar of their own cars. This is reminiscent of the old days, when a traveller was prepared to sell his own horse if someone was prepared to buy it.

"A lot of people live in trailer parks in their own vans. Mobile homes are a lot cheaper, and are a better class out there. If things go wrong, or a man is made redundant, they can just pack up and move on until they find work somewhere else." John explained.

A traveller family wedding draws relatives and friends together from all over the world, and on visits to Canada, John has become aware of how his relatives have become respected and prominent citizens in their communities. "My people being Canadian travellers are well known in lots of states and well liked and respected wherever they do business." He was not required to show his passport at the bank across the road from his cousin's trailer park, when he went to change some English currency into dollars. The fact that he was attending a Townsley wedding was all that the bank needed to know. "My cousin was one of the bank's best clients."

During the long holiday that they spent in the country, John and Kath were able to

137

visit many of their relatives, many of whom were previously unknown to them, yet, *"They could tell me where every one of the Townsleys was living, and what business every one was operating. Some live in luxurious surroundings with their own swimming pools, ballrooms in their houses and plenty of land surrounding their properties if the need arises to extend their homes."*

One of the sports that the North American members of the Clan enjoy is reminiscent of the days in the "old country", when travellers used to gather at an appointed time on lonely moor roads of the north of England, to race against each other in their horse and trap. While the sport of trotting is still carried out in some parts of the British Isles, in Canada and the USA, the sport has the additional extravagance and glamour that the North Americans bring to their sporting occasions.

"When we were over in Canada, we used to go to the trotting stadium in Toronto, and also to the one in London Ontario. They were just fantastic and had everything. We also went to the new six storey high trotting stadium in Cicero, Chicago. You could go to any level on the lifts or escalators. There were lounges for drinks, restaurants, beauty parlours, massage and sauna baths, shops and inside and outside viewing areas. The trotting there started at eight o clock in the evening, and the last race took place at twelve thirty. These trotting races were held every night in the summer, and during the winter time, the horses were sent away to Florida. It was just out of this world."

If family weddings draw travellers together from all over the world, then family funerals have the same effect. To many people, some of the Gypsy funerals may seem extravagant affairs, for the the cost of the flowers alone can reach a five figure sum. Robert Kelly, of Malton in Yorkshire, is, as far as he is aware, the only recognised Romany florist in the country. *"You need to be aware of the traditions, and the order that the floral tributes follow. All the tributes are about three to four feet high, and they are made to stand up. They are mounted on flat wagons, that follow the coffin and the number of tributes directly reflects the Gypsy's standing in the hierarchy of the community. The procession of a large Gypsy funeral can bring a town to a halt."*

Robert explained that the tribute that immediately follows the coffin is that of a full length cross which completely covers the coffin, and is always from the next of kin. The next tribute, in the case of an old person is from the eldest son or daughter and is in the form of an empty chair. In some cases, Robert has actually used the Gypsy's favourite chair and covered it with flowers and foliage. Next in order of precedence comes an arrangement representing the "Gates of Heaven" to signify the passing of the Gypsy into life beyond the grave. Then comes a floral harp, with a broken string, or a broken wheel that denote the break in the family line, If the Gypsy was a horse dealer, a creation of a floral horse's head complete with a bridle will feature among the tributes. The young people and children among the Gypsy's relatives and friends will send small floral tributes that reflect the Gypsy's life-style and can include such ordinary items as packets of cigarettes, or even cans of his favourite beer. *"The decoration, and the design of the floral tributes actually reflect the Gypsy's life"* said Robert.

Tales of a Lakeland Gypsy

One such funeral followed a tragedy that befell some of John's relatives in Canada.

"My cousin Betty Townsley married Tom Forrest. He was on the tarmac job and they were on the camp at Calgary. Their boys had been out working in the van, and when they came back, they gave their mother the ROWDY they had made that day, had something to eat, got washed and changed to go into Calgary to one of the discos." The boys decided not to go in their own vehicle, but accompany some friends in their car. Instead of driving along the highway, which was the normal route into Calgary, they drove out along a dirt road.

"The road crosses the railway line at a sort of switch back. The Vancouver Express was running late that night; it ploughed into the car on the crossing and the boys were all killed. They flew the boys back to England in caskets to Heathrow, for them to be buried in England at Banbury in Oxfordshire. There was dealers and friends from all over the world. The memorial was a black marble altar, with large black bibles in black marble and pictures of the boys in black marble frames. This was a tragic loss for these were the only two boys in all of the Forest families."

If the Winter family were powerful in the area round Ontario, then in the Toronto region it was Abel Boyd and his family who held sway.

"Abel Boyd was my mother's full cousin. He had sixteen of a family and at home ran a carting business and was a horse dealer. He was one of the big wheels in the travelling fraternity. He emigrated to Canada in the 1800's. He built a reputation as a horse dealer that railroaded thousand of horses to points all over Canada. At one time he had the sole rights to supply horses to the Canadian Mounted Police. He also had a large yard where he would buy and sell anything that was saleable. Travellers used to gather in the yard to talk just as they did at home."

On one occasion, some business men came into Abel Boyd's yard. They had travelled all the way across country and called in to pass on news of what was happening on the other side of the country. This was an important contact, for Abel and his family used to send horses by rail, across country to be sold in the Vancouver auction ring, where they were in partnership with the auctioneer. Through his conversation with the visitors to the yard, Abel quickly realised that the prices for which some of the horses were sold did not tally with the price that he was receiving from his partner.

"Abel was a dollar millionaire by then, but he sent a telegram to his partner to get squared up. Most of his money was tied up in bonds and he had not the ready cash to lose on the horses he had sent, or to buy new ones. A week later, the cheque arrived and Abel took it to the bank where he asked for it to be cashed into dollars. When Abel Boyd grafts, he grafts for himself, not for FLATTYS in Vancouver. Abel was a master at the YAGGING game, especially where there was considerable sums of ROWDY or goods involved."

Another travelling family was the Lightfoots whose ancestors had also emigrated from Scotland to follow a travelling way of life in their new country. They probably spent more time in following the traditional life-style than did any of the other traveller

139

families, but they eventually settled down in the Montreal area and opened shops and a warehouse from where many other travellers were supplied with their goods. Members of all the families that includes the Townsleys, the Winters, the Boyds, and the Lightfoots still keep up their links with their relatives in the "old country."

Although among these relatives, there are many that John has never seen, Christmas cards and letters keep them all in touch, and the traditions that are embedded in them through family tales, ensure a continuing contact with the country they regard as home. *"Although we have never met, there's something special about the breed. Some of them will write and say, this will be Appleby Fair time, or the crocus will be coming through, and all the other thing's that happen with the seasons in nature's countryside. Although a lot of them have never been to this country, they still remember everything their parents told them about the old country."*

The young Townsleys who worked their way through Canada.
From L - R, Charlie, Tom and Jamesy.

APPENDIX - ROMANY LANGUAGE

The language spoken by Romanies or Gypsies, is known as Cant. John Townsley explained that it is his understanding that many of the words are Gaelic or Eastern in origin. As with the language of many other cultures, some of the words have been absorbed into the English language.

John explained that when Gypsies are involved in deals with non -Gypsies, or FLATTIES, it was particularly useful to be able to converse with one's own people in a way that was not understood by others.

John Townsley is still able to speak Cant, and some of those words slip quite naturally into his everyday vocabulary. It was inevitable that in the telling of the tales, some Cant words would occur. The context in which they are used is often sufficient to give an explanation of the meaning, while for others, this appended short glossary may prove to be both useful and interesting.

● ●

Cant - English

barry - good
barry tuggery - good old clothes
blackies - coal
blood stick - carrying little weight
bool - rim of a bowl, a frame strengthener
buck - half bred traveller
bunce -

chanters - singers
cha - tea
chiney - sugar
chitties - iron tripod chain hooks over camp fire
chorey - stolen goods
cleek - iron hook
cold shouldered - work shy
coorie - snuggle in
crine - shrink

crab it - condemn it
crown - five shillings
cushty - good
cuddy - donkey
cushty duke - platignum

dander - a short stroll
donat - lazy
dropping - giving birth
drumly - disturbed, confused
ducals - dogs
duckering - fortune telling
dude - milk
duke - metal
dunage - scrap

esh plant - cosh stick

141

fallage - a word of expression, different meaning implied by intonation and emphasis
fam - hand
fash - to worry
fassom - hair
feeking - at own price
flatties - ordinary folk, outsider
flute - suit
fonk - smell

garron - a highland horse
go nash - scarpered
gouger - ordinary person
gel - let's go
gilt - money
groins - rings with stones
gruffys - pigs

hogg - a shilling

iffy - not legally gained
iron crook - a boiling kettle

jiggers - doors

keks - trousers
kens - homes

lag - passing water
lag ken - toilet, urinal
larey - cunning
long tails - vermin
lum - chimney
luvre - money

mass - meat
manisher - woman
mark - a deal
midden - muck heap
milly - shirt
misfits - not genuine

moy - mouth
muffler - scarf
musker - police

nark - informer
nattlers - bones
nappy - gammy, runaway
neeps - turnip

old rust - jewellery
old stuff - scrap
oxter - armpit

paggering - beating
pancrackers - dole men
pareys - fleas
peesie - peewit
peevers - pubs
plotes - feet
poke - small bag
pongo - linoleum
proven- horse feed
puckle - a little

radgie - daft
raffie - someone to be exploited, a "mug"
red mass - copper
red rudd - rubbing stones
rocks - rings with stones
rooty - bread
rosie - precious metal
rowdy - money
runners - pheasants/partridge

scams- dodgy deals
scran - food
scuffs - hats
scull - wicker basket
slappy - butter
stall - hang back
stardy - a prison sentence
stoor - dust

swag - rugs, mats, clothes
switchers - rabbits

tats - woollens for goldfish
the silver - mercury
tuavas [pronounce chavas] - grown up
    children
tuggery - clothes

vardo - caravan

waxy - linoleum

yags - coals
yaggers - colliers
yak - eye
yellow cowie - brass
yoke - horse cart

Remembering the old days.

The Anglers Inn, Ennerdale.

The Hill, Appleby Fair.